The Process Approach

of

ISO 9001

by T. D. Nelson

The Process Approach of ISO 9001 by T. D. Nelson

Copyright © 2015 by T.D. Nelson

First Printing: April 2014

Second Edition: May 2014

Third Edition: October 2015

Fourth Edition: January 2016

Printed in the United States of America

This book is dedicated to any who struggle with the requirements of ISO 9001. The struggle stops with an understanding of the process approach and how it relates to systemic quality management. After that, ISO 9001 is easy.

Thank you to those who helped with this book, including Paul Harding, Noel Wilson, Ellen Kehoe, Fred Walker, Jim Hehlke, David Hoyle, Mo Nelson (no relation), Paul Simpson, and an anonymous reviewer at the American Society for Quality (ASQ). A special thanks to Colin Gray for teaching me about the process approach.

(Please note: views presented in this book do not necessarily reflect the views of those credited above.)

Foreword

Dan Nelson is passionate about promoting the use of the "process approach" when using ISO 9001 and so he should be.

He is not a voice alone when it comes to this topic but few people share his passion. However, are his views shared by the majority of the standard users around the world? The sad reality is that most of the management system implementers and auditors that use ISO 9001:2008 have adopted a "standard-based" approach rather than a "process-based" approach. This book goes a long way to explain the difference between the two approaches.

If you watch a football game, are two games ever the same? The answer is of course no. However, do the games follow the same rules? The answer is of course yes. The point of this book is to explain that "the game" should fall within the "rules" as laid down in the standard and not focus on the "rules" themselves. If all the "rules" are followed no one would even notice that the rules existed. Each game is made up of a series of interacting processes and players. Those processes themselves do not happen by accident. The coach will spend hours perfecting those processes as well as the application of them by the players. If the coach is good, a winning team will be the result and the spectators (customers) will be satisfied.

Paul Harding, Managing Director, South African Quality Institute

Introduction

In the above picture, one can see a haggard old woman and a lovely young woman. Sure, it may be more natural for a viewer to see one or the other, but with a little effort and a change in perspective, two different images appear in this one illustration. It seems natural for the mind to entertain only one image at a time, doesn't it?

It's this kind of image illusion that has stymied proper understanding of ISO 9001 since its original release. ISO 9001 has developed a bad image due to a poor understanding of the standard and what it actually requires.

ISO 9001 appears to many as the haggard old woman. For years, an incorrect image of what ISO 9001 requires has been widely projected by professionals in the industry, promoting an old-school, ineffective way of applying ISO 9001.

The beauty in ISO 9001 cannot be seen from this perspective. The lovely young woman is standing right before us, yet so few see her.

The Process Approach of ISO 9001

Seeing the beauty of ISO 9001 comes with an understanding of the process approach, but this understanding escapes those who insist upon seeing the old hag.

Hopefully this book will help promote a change in perspective, imparting an appreciation for the beauty in ISO 9001. Understanding the process approach is key.

A Problem with ISO 9001

If you use a power tool contrary to its manufacturer's recommendations and you experience bad results, do you blame the tool? Do you blame the manufacturer? If you were dissatisfied with a tool, yet you continue to use it without reading the instructions—and continue to experience bad results—wouldn't you at some point begin to wonder if you should properly understand the manufacturers' recommendations?

The most damning pitfall associated with ISO 9001 is a matter of basic approach. For decades, an errant, old-school approach was widely purported to be required of the standard itself. Though generally accepted today, this was never true. In reality, it's an awful solution for organizations trying to manage quality.

The unhappy, ironic result: in an effort to become certified to an international quality standard, many organizations adopted a poor approach to quality management. Meanwhile, as management is reducing costs in every way possible, the unnecessary overhead built into quality management systems (QMSs) goes unrecognized. It's unwittingly accepted as a cost of doing business.

If organizations are to gain value from their QMSs, the prevalent old-school approach needs to be abolished in favor of the process approach. Until then, the value of ISO 9001 will continue to elude organizations.

If your organization is like many who have become certified to ISO 9001, quality management may seem confusing. Unfortunately, ISO 9001 is too often misapplied to businesses using a fundamentally bad approach that makes no sense, often adds piles of paperwork, complicates business operations with poorly-defined processes that add no value to the bottom line, creates confusion among personnel, and hinders quality. This approach is a one-size-fits-all plan that shoehorns every business into the same clunky, cumbersome model that disregards the individuality of any organization or industry sector. Companies that use this backward approach to ISO 9001 restructure the definition of their business processes into a counterintuitive arrangement that obscures processes and makes managing quality more difficult than it was before—hence the widespread disdain for ISO 9001.

Evidenced by the dwindling number of ISO 9001 certificates being issued in many parts of the world, many organizations dislike ISO 9001. Organizations commonly find ISO 9001 to be confusing and somewhat painful, while at the same time requiring odd documentation seemingly only understood by consultants and auditors. Unaware that ISO 9001 has been improperly applied in their organizations, personnel question the value of the standard itself. After all, they implemented and followed the consultant's pre-written procedures to a tee, and external auditors confirmed that they had correctly applied the standard. Yet these systems, drawing accolades from consultants and auditors, seem dysfunctional to sensible management personnel. No wonder they don't like ISO 9001.

The Real Problem: A Misunderstanding

The process approach is a concept crucial to proper quality management. This concept is not new. In fact, it's how ISO 9001 was designed to work from the very beginning. A process approach allows businesses to realize the full benefit of a management system by viewing and managing real processes affecting the quality of products and services offered to customers. The more prevalent standard-based approach, as opposed to a process approach, was born of a small misunderstanding that grew larger as a snowball effect overtook the ISO 9000 world. Businesses followed bad examples, and the problem grew larger. Incorrectly applying ISO 9001 requirements became the norm.

The Process Approach of ISO 9001

The misunderstanding is simple. ISO 9001 was never intended to tell management how to manage. It never purported to contain instructions for how to run a business. It was merely intended to provide auditors with a consistent set of criteria with which to assess QMSs. It's a set of quality principles meted out in specific requirements, intended to provide a basis for consistent, fair assessment. Businesses have applied ISO 9001 in such a fundamentally incorrect manner—focusing on conformity to ISO 9001 instead of focusing on their own quality management—that the purpose, value, and intent of ISO 9001 have been defeated.

The original version of ISO 9001 was very clearly intended as audit criteria. Of course nobody was supposed to write 20 procedures pandering to the 20 elements of the standard and call the resulting mess a QMS. ISO 9001 was not supposed to be implemented as a QMS by management; it was supposed to be applied as audit criteria by auditors. Yet clearly most organizations used it to "implement their QMSs"—evidenced by the same 20 standard-based procedures defining the management systems of thousands and thousands of organizations.

The intended audience of ISO 9001—auditors—often promoted the idea that the standard was intended for use by management. "Here, management, these requirements are for you to implement, we'll check back later to see how well your procedures match" as opposed to "Here, management, these requirements are what you will be assessed against, we'll use them to see if your system conforms." The former urges management to implement ISO 9001; the latter hopes management will implement a system that complies with ISO 9001, or, more accurately, they will document the existing system as it is implemented and enhance it as necessary to meet the requirements of ISO 9001. ISO 9001 is an assessment tool.

Incorrectly thinking that they were the proper audience of ISO 9001, management developed standard-based systems of 20 procedures to address ISO 9001:1987/1994 requirements. Specific requirements were subsumed beneath 20 general elements, while each element called for documented procedures addressing its requirements (thus allowing objective definition appropriate for assessment). A standard-based mindset concludes that the standard required 20 procedures—one for each element—to satisfy the requirements for documented procedures.

A process-based mindset, on the other hand, concludes that documented procedures—whatever their number—must address the requirements of the 20 elements. So, an organization operating 10 processes would document those processes using 10 procedures—one for each process. These 10 procedures would need to appropriately address the requirements of the 20 elements as they apply to the defined 10 processes. So, many were confused about who the implementers of ISO 9001 really were. ISO 9001 is supposed to be implemented to assess QMSs. It was not intended for use by management to structure QMSs. Organizational management were not supposed to be the implementers of ISO 9001; they were often confused about how to apply ISO 9001.

Based on user survey results and observations of widespread misuse of the standard, the authors of the 2000 standard recognized organizations were often using ISO 9001 to establish their QMSs. So many of them were doing it that way, ISO seemed to accept this new group of unintended customers. "Since that's how our product is being used," the thinking seemed to go, "then we must respond to the demands of these unintended, uniformed customers."

In response to survey results and feedback, ISO seemed to acknowledge that its "customers" were using the standard to develop QMSs. ISO seemed to rise to the occasion and cater to this previously unintended audience. With the 2000 revision of ISO 9001, the authors of the standard seemed to do two things: one, they made a move toward addressing this new audience, while two, they tried to make it clear that the standard requires a process approach. "If organizations are going to use ISO 9001 as the basis of their systems, okay—but they must be clear that the standard is supposed to be applied using a process approach."

Apparently resigned to the fact that management was going to use the standard as a basis for QMS design, the authors did what they could to promote application of a process approach by an audience with a standard-based mindset. The first attempt to stymie a standard-based mindset in the 2000 standard is in its introduction (ISO 9001:2000, 0.1), where it tells us that it is NOT the intent of the standard to compel uniform QMS structure and documentation (e.g., by using it as a foundation for QMS definition).

Then at "0.2, Process approach" the standard explains that plan-do-check-act (PDCA) is the basis of the process approach. The supposition is that QMSs will be structured with PDCA in mind, not with the uniform requirements of ISO 9001 in mind. Process-based procedures describe processes: the proper subject of PDCA application. A process-based procedure represents the plan for processing pursuant to the "Plan" phase of PDCA; a standard-based procedure is merely written in response to an ISO 9001 requirement. Procedures raised in response to ISO 9001 requirements cannot effectively describe the plan for any core business process. Merely describing conformity with individual ISO 9001 requirements, standard-based procedures offer the DCA phases of PDCA no real basis upon which to operate. From an organizational perspective, PDCA operates on processes, not requirements.

Then at 4.1, the standard provides requirements presumed adequate to determine if a defined system demonstrates a process approach. However, the requirements at 4.1 were apparently not adequate to overcome the standard-based mindset. Many read the standard to mean that only six procedures were required to define a QMS, since there were now only six requirements expressly calling for documented procedures (basically to cover support processes).

If organizations were going to use the standard to raise QMSs, the authors seemed to think that an admonishment against the standard-based approach (0.1), an endorsement of the process approach (0.2), followed by requirements effectively demanding a process approach (4.1) would solve the problem. Since 2000, the intent of the standard could be construed to include QMS development guidance as demanded by the originally unintended users. It could now, in a sense, speak to those who think they need it to define their management systems. Now we hear of ISO 9001-based QMSs with justification from ISO. But ISO 9001 does not offer justification to use the standard as a clause-by-clause or six-procedure-only basis for any QMS. So, the 2015 standard will continue to clarify and emphasize the requirement to apply a process approach.

After the year 2000, organizations simply took the reduced emphasis on documentation to mean that a QMS needed less documentation-- from 20 procedures down to six. However, a good QMS may have been defined by only 10 procedures under 1994, thus already having reduced documentation from that needed by the conventional 20-procedure wisdom. When the standard reduced emphasis on documentation in 2000, a system previously defined by 10 procedures is still defined by 10 procedures. Definition of the system and its processes does not depend on ISO 9001, nor should documentation describing a defined system. No system was ever properly defined by 20 standard-based procedures or merely by the "six mandatory" procedures.

To overcome the standard-based mindset, it seems it was a mistake to allow the inmates to take over the asylum. ISO seems to have shot itself in the foot trying to achieve customer satisfaction—catering to customers who were misapplying the standard. With the release of ISO 9001:2000, it's as if ISO was saying:

"Okay, if you all insist on using this standard for assessing QMSs to establish QMSs, which is actually very cheeky cheating, then we are including a requirement to apply a process approach. So, if an organization uses ISO 9001 as a basis for its QMS, management can't miss this endorsement of, and requirement to apply, a process approach. We are reducing the emphasis on documentation to make it more clear that this exercise is not merely about writing voluminous documentation to claim conformity with the individual requirements of the standard, as has been done thus far. Nobody liked that documentation, nor should they have, it was misguided and not required in the first place. So, an ISO 9001-based QMS will be a process-based QMS—documented according to operations, not according to the requirements of ISO 9001."

The Process Approach of ISO 9001

What everyone seemed to hear: "The process approach only requires six procedures, but our clause-by-clause procedures are still okay."

It seems trouble can be expected anytime a simple, organic concept becomes codified and institutionalized. Quality management in a structured way is supposed to be all about "plan-do-check-act" (PDCA). Simply, PDCA is a WAY of managing. But when it becomes a discrete requirement couched in technical terms of an international standard (e.g., "process," "system," "procedure," requirement,"), the risk of misapplying it appears to be greater than many appreciate.

Part of the reason why this misunderstanding managed to take root so firmly in the ISO world: the haste to get certified put management in a situation where they needed to move quickly, but not really understanding ISO 9001, it was unclear what needed to be done. They turned to ISO consultants for help. ISO consultants, often steeped in a standard-based mind-set, provided each client organization with pre-written documents based on the standard, rather than simply documenting what each organization did for a living. How can pre-written documents describe operations of any company? They can't. But organizations were often erroneously told these documents were required of the standard.

So, organizations largely viewed ISO 9001 as a necessary evil, a documentation burden that had to be borne whether they liked it or not. Under pressure to implement on a tight timeline and keep costs low, management failed to understand the true objective of a formal management system. Without information about the process approach to guide them in the right direction, the temptation to use pre-written, off-the-shelf documentation went unchecked. Using canned documentation appeared to be the shortest path to the goal. Nothing could have been further from the truth. Of course, the goal is much further down the road than just ISO 9001 certification. The goal is to implement sensible, systemic quality management first, after which ISO 9001 certification will follow.

Look at it this way: ISO 9001 certification is a test. Third-party, certifying body (CB) auditors proctor the test. The criteria of the exam are widely published. The test is no secret; it's "open book." The idea is not to pass the test by adopting documentation pandering to the exam criteria, or by copying it from others who achieved certification (using others' passing test papers). In any other field, that would be viewed as cheating and corrupt.

What is the objective of cheating? Cheating is usually intended to be a shortcut or a way to avoid the expense and inconvenience that comes with not cheating. But those who have adopted a standard-based approach—in their attempt to take a shortcut—have actually tied up more resources and incurred more expense than the process approach would ever have required.

Trying to outwit an old hag, organizations actually chose the hard route and it's costing them plenty. She's a bright young lady and she demands respect. Properly understood and respected, she's a very sensible lady.

ISO 9001 demands a process approach. That's good news for organizations. Not only is it easier for organizations to deal with—and imperative from a quality management perspective—but proper application of its requirements presupposes it. Failure to understand the process approach often results in misapplication of the standard, virtually ensuring a miserable experience with the resulting QMS. This is awful not only because it's unnecessary, but because it drains resources from the organization while at the same time damaging the organizational concept of quality management. It hasn't done much for the reputations of ISO 9001 or the quality professionals involved with it, either.

There is a solution, of course, and that's what this book is about. If your company has applied ISO 9001 using a bad approach and you want to start experiencing the real power of ISO 9001, this book will show you a framework for re-aligning your processes to take advantage of your QMS. If you are seeking certification for the first time, this book will help you understand how to follow the right path and avoid the pitfalls of using a bad approach.

The Process Approach of ISO 9001

W. Edwards Deming

Before diving into the thick of ISO 9001, here is some background context about one of the pioneers of what has become the modern-day process-based approach: W. Edwards Deming.

By the late 80s, it became apparent that Japanese cars were in many ways superior to their American counterparts. They were often more reliable and durable and they got better gas mileage. They were of superior quality. They often still are. To what do the Japanese attribute their success? The teachings of W. Edwards Deming. The Japanese listened to Deming when Americans would not.

Deming introduced the idea that the best way to assure product quality was to assure the quality of the processes that create product. The focus isn't so much upon product, but how product is created. Deming was focused upon processes and process management. Akin to the old adage, "Mind your pennies and your dollars will take care of themselves," Deming seemed to be saying, "Mind your processes and quality will take care of itself," or, "Mind your quality and your business will take care of itself."

In the 1940s, Deming's focus on process management as a long-term solution to organizational profitability and stability was viewed by American management as being unprofitable. Ignored at home, Deming took his show on the road. After World War II, Deming was among a team of professionals who went to Japan to help rebuild their economy after the war. Deming told the Japanese that if they would listen to him, they would become an economic powerhouse in the global economy.

I was a kid during the 70s. I remember when "Made in Japan" was virtually synonymous with "junk." Yet by the mid 80s, true to Deming's alleged timeframe prediction, "Made in Japan" was nothing to scoff at. Today, Japanese quality is superb. It's not just cars and trucks, either. Look at their electronics, too. Today, "Made in Japan" means "quality stuff." The Japanese import raw materials, make product, and export it (even paying tariffs), and these products now consistently outperform competitors in the global market.

More than a quality guru, Deming was a business guru. The Japanese prove it every day. I don't believe that American industry is ignoring Deming's teachings on purpose, but many ISO 9001-certified organizations are ignoring Deming with the very systems they have raised to pass ISO 9001 audits. In an effort to become ISO 9001 certified, organizations have adopted an approach that neglects the most critical processes to any QMS.

The Science behind PDCA

Today, PDCA is widely known as the Deming cycle. However, Deming himself called it the Shewhart cycle, in deference to his mentor, Walter Shewhart. Shewhart introduced an early version of the model in his 1939 book, *Statistical Method from the Viewpoint of Quality Control.* Deming added to it, introducing it to the Japanese as PDSA (plan-do-study-act). The Japanese called it the "Deming wheel." So Deming popularized PDCA. Arriving at PDCA itself appears to have been an iterative, collaborative process involving Shewhart, Deming and others.

While the thinking that resulted in today's PDCA can be most immediately traced to Shewhart's 1939 book, these underpinnings themselves had underpinnings. Insight into the history of PDCA is offered by an article titled "Circling Back" (Ronald D. Moen and Clifford L. Norman, Quality Progress, November, 2010). The article can be found here:

http://asq.org/quality-progress/2010/11/basic-quality/circling-back.html

According to "Circling Back," the history of PDCA can be traced back through a lineage of pragmatic and scientific thinkers: C.I. Lewis, John Dewey, Charles Pierce, William James, Sir Francis Bacon, and Galileo—the father of modern science. (We might trace the idea all the way back to Socrates for that matter.) In a sense, when Shewhart arrived at the beginnings of PDCA, he was applying scientific method to the production methods of his day.

The Process Approach of ISO 9001

PDCA resembles scientific method, if you think about it. It's a system of acquiring new knowledge, or improving upon or integrating what was previously known into current practice.

Here's a rough depiction of scientific method:

1. **Hypothesis** (stated explanation of reality),
2. **Test** the hypothesis (via application or experiment),
3. **Evaluate** the hypothesis (evaluate its explanatory power or accuracy), and
4. **Adjust** (or abandon) the hypothesis if it fails to explain reality. If adjusted, repeat the cycle. If the hypothesis satisfactorily explains, it is accepted and perhaps tested elsewhere.

In the context of a quality management system, the scientific method of PDCA can be illustrated as follows.

1. **Plan** (hypothesis: this plan for processing will achieve process objectives),
2. **Do** (test hypothesis: implement the plan, do it according to plan),
3. **Check** (evaluate hypothesis: determine the degree to which the implemented plan achieved objectives), and
4. **Act** (adjust the hypothesis: make improvements to the plan in order to improve performance as desired). If performance needs to improve, action is taken to improve the system, or else improvement cannot be expected. If performance is acceptable, the plan is good. Follow the plan.

Being clear about a plan is important if actions to improve the plan are to be effective. In the case of a QMS procedure, the procedure describes the plan for carrying out a process. The procedure needs to be clear enough to ensure whatever level of consistency is needed for the process to be considered stable (during the *do* phase). Once somewhat stable, process performance measures (applied during the *check* phase) offer value in deciding where improvements can or need to be made. Based on sound performance measures, management makes sound decisions about how to improve performance (during the *act* phase).

Some folks seem to think of quality as just a warm fuzzy, feel-good thing. While it may be that, too, there is cold, hard science beneath it. It's where scientific method meets everyday operations.

Shewhart's basic idea seems to have involved viewing a process as an iterative cycle, rather than viewing it as something linear, something that finishes at the end. Viewed simply as a prescribed, linear sequence of activities, the process objective becomes to simply "get it done." When a process is viewed as being finished upon delivery of outputs (after completion of the *do* phase of PDCA), no consideration might be given to process effectiveness and efficiency or to future processing. Being finished, the process merely awaits its next inputs, which are to be processed just like the previous inputs were. A linear, static process like this will not improve itself. It takes informed action to improve a process.

Viewed as an iterative cycle, a process is improved between cycles. A process isn't over after the *do* phase. There is still the *check* and *act* phases. Of course, if previous performance were perfect, then improvement wouldn't be possible. Otherwise, however, there's room for improvement. Based on performance information, management chooses what's important to improve upon and what isn't. The basic idea is to routinely improve processes performance, a simple concept that comes naturally to management.

My Background

I originally learned the process approach in 1998 from a Brit named Colin. He had been using a process approach with British Standard 5750 (BS 5750), the precursor to ISO 9001. By 1987, when ISO 9001 was released, Colin was an old hand.

Prior to being enlightened by Colin, I thought the standard required twenty procedures, one for each element of the standard. This was widely espoused by ISO 9001 professionals—consultants, book authors, and auditors alike. Everyone I knew who was in the know said so. It wasn't even a question. Although this approach was and continues to be accepted, it is neither best practice nor acceptable according to good sense, good management, or good quality assurance—it doesn't even make sense according to the standard itself.

After learning the process approach, I used it exclusively to establish QMSs for scores of organizations of various sizes and in various industries and to fix dysfunctional systems (to the delight of customers). They pass ISO 9001 audits with flying colors, too. In 1998, we didn't have a name for this approach. Colin and I referred to it simply as "the right way." When ISO 9001:2000 was released, our "right way" was given a name: the process approach.

Had organizations been using a process approach consistently up until 2000, the requirements to use a process approach would not have appeared in the 2000 standard. But the presupposed process approach went overlooked by those steeped in a standard-based mind-set. After 2000, consultants continued churning out standard-based solutions (i.e., canned manuals and procedures responding to ISO 9001 requirements), while auditors continued accepting them. Common though they are, standard-based solutions contradict a process approach.

If organizations were consistently using a process approach today, the requirement to use a process approach would not be emphasized as expected in the upcoming revision of ISO 9001. In other words, the problem is still going strong.

Good News and Bad News
Bad News First…

Many people dislike ISO 9001. Those working in organizations certified to an ISO 9001-based standard—ISO 13485, ISO/TS16949, AS9100, etc.—often harbor disdain for ISO 9001 and those involved with it. This book hopes to accomplish two things: 1) clarify that the standard is not the problem, and 2) suggest how to fix the problem at an organizational level.

The bad news: if your organization is certified to ISO 9001, chances are good that you have fallen victim to a bad idea. It is very widespread and common, even today. When organizations dislike ISO 9001, it's often because they are approaching it wrong.

It's easy to tell if this bad idea lurks in your organization. Simply look at your QMS procedures and supporting documentation. If your system includes documents carrying any of the following titles, your QMS may be suffering from the affliction that this book is designed to address.

Examples include, but are not limited to:

- "Product Identification" or "Production Identification and Traceability"
- "Inspection and Test" or "Inspection and Test Status"
- "Customer Property"
- "Customer-Supplied Product"
- "Preservation of Product"
- "Handling, Storage, Packaging, Preservation, and Delivery"

If any of these titles sound familiar, this book is for you—and you're by no means alone. This book is also for anyone whose QMS procedures consist only of those raised in response to the six ISO 9001 requirements clearly calling for documented procedures: document control, record control, internal audits, nonconforming product, corrective action, and preventive action. These six were meant to be generic for every organization plus whatever processes your unique organization carries out.

While this book is dedicated to a discussion of ISO 9001 and the process approach, the same principles pertain to sector schemes, e.g. ISO/TS 16949 for the automobile industry, or ISO 13485 for the medical device industry, or AS9100 for the aerospace industry. Apparently no sectors were immune to this bad approach.

The Process Approach of ISO 9001

Now the Good News...

ISO 9001 is much easier and more sensible than you might have thought. For decades, many in the ISO 9001 business have been demanding that processes conform to a bad idea, adding piles of senseless documentation, needlessly complicating workflows, and creating confusion within businesses about what quality assurance is. From the perspective of quality management, the process approach aligns with common-sense management principles that intuitively make sense to management. Companies that implement the process approach find that QMSs align naturally with the way they managed processes before ISO 9001 came along. That's how ISO was intended to work.

Properly applied, a concept endorsed by the standard itself will result in quality making sense again and it will spare management needless headaches by eliminating useless documentation. Using the process approach, time spent training personnel to understand confusing procedures will be recouped. Costs of administrating unneeded documents will be avoided (e.g. revising, reviewing, approving, and distributing them), while also avoiding the added expense of auditing documents that never should have been drafted in the first place.

Is There Quality in Your QMS?

ISO 9000 Basics

ISO 9000 is a family of documents. One document in the family is ISO 9000 itself, which lays out fundamental principles behind the standard and defines terms used within the family.

A second document in the family is the international standard for quality management systems: ISO 9001. ISO 9001 contains requirements against which organizations' QMSs are assessed. Those demonstrating conformity to all requirements are granted registration (or certification) to ISO 9001.

ISO 9004 is a third document in the family. It provides guidance for sustained success beyond the basic requirements contained in ISO 9001.

In this book, and as is common in the industry, "ISO 9000" is used casually to mean the whole family of documents, while a more precise usage of the term would concern only the ISO 9000 document. When the term "ISO 9001" is used, it is to designate the requirements document specifically.

External, independent CBs, or registrars, are accredited by an accreditation body and are responsible for granting ISO 9001 registrations. CB auditors assess QMSs and make recommendations as to whether QMSs should be certified; CBs make registration decisions largely based upon these recommendations.

The most current revision of ISO 9001 was released in 2015, (ISO 9001:2015). Since its original release in 1987, there have been four revisions: 1994, 2000, 2008, and 2015. Changes in requirements between the 1987 and the 1994 standards were minor. The 2000 revision contained many requirements similar to those of the 1987/1994 revisions, but the format changed drastically including adoption of the PDCA cycle—and it began to emphasize documented procedures in a fundamentally different way. It also expressly demanded a process approach. But nobody seemed to notice. Again, the changes between the 2000 and 2008 revisions were minor. ISO 2015 represents another major rearrangement of the standard's structure, though most requirements have again merely been re-voiced to keep up with the times.

The process approach is not a new idea. In fact, ISO 9001 always assumed that organizations would use a process approach to raise QMSs. But ISO 9001:2000 was the first revision that explicitly said so, dedicating a section to it (0.2, Process approach). The first effective requirements of the standard (4.1, General requirements), require a process approach. Each of the seven requirements within 4.1 pertain to QMS processes—identifying the processes affecting quality, determining their sequence and interaction, monitoring these processes, managing these processes, etc. One might get the idea that it's all about processes—managing processes, controlling processes and improving processes—which it is. That's a big part of what quality management is all about.

A Taste of the Process Approach

To understand the process approach, it's useful to contrast it with a more common approach. This common approach is what Colin and I used to call "the wrong way," or, "the standard approach." "Standard" here has a double meaning: standard as in routine or customary, and standard as in relying upon a standard to identify and document organizational processes. Today, it is becoming known as "the standard-based approach." It gets its moniker from the idea that QMSs are properly structured and documented according to the requirements, clauses, or sub-clauses of the standard(s) to which organizations seek certification.

To illustrate the difference between a process approach and a standard-based approach, let's take the case of a hypothetical small manufacturing company, called Bob's Machine Shop, which builds product to customer specification. In this company, five processes directly affect quality: Sales, Purchasing, Receiving, Production, and Shipping. Absent one of these processes, the company could not deliver quality product to customers. So these are processes necessary for the company's QMS. Think of them as being top-level processes (or management system processes).

1. Sales process—review customer requirements and accept orders

2. Purchasing process—procure tools and materials needed to manufacture product

3. Receiving process—receive and verify that incoming goods meet purchasing requirements

4. Production process—manufacture final product to customer specifications

5. Shipping process—package product and ship to customer

Using a standard-based approach, Bob's Machine Shop can buy pre-written procedures needed to demonstrate conformity to the standard on a store shelf or online. The structure and content of these procedures are predetermined by the standard itself. This is a one-size-fits-all approach. Organizational processes are not even considered in the architecture of the system or its procedures. It's like giving every organization the same bad bowl haircut. The popular "ISO" cut.

As you may remember, up until the 2000 revision replaced the 1994 revision, most organizations would become registered to ISO 9001 or ISO 9002—depending on what they did for a living. ISO 9001:1994 was for organizations that designed and manufactured their product while ISO 9002:1994 was for organizations manufacturing product to customer design and specification. (ISO 9002 was simply ISO 9001 with the design requirements, element 4.4, omitted.)

Today, organizations become registered to ISO 9001. If certain requirements do not apply to an organization's QMS—specifically those residing in section 7 of the 2000/2008 standards—the organization excludes the requirements. These are known as permissible exclusions. So, a contract manufacturer that is not design-responsible receives certification to ISO 9001:2008, just the same as a manufacturer that is design-responsible. The contract manufacturer simply excludes the design requirements, justifying the exclusion within the quality manual (where the scope of the QMS is defined).

The Process Approach of ISO 9001

In our example, under the 1994 scheme, Bob's Machine Shop would seek certification to ISO 9002:1994, since it builds to customer specification (and is not design-responsible). Since the company doesn't offer servicing agreements, another of the requirements is not applicable: 4.19, Servicing. Both 4.19 and 4.4, Design, are omitted. Eighteen requirements remain applicable to the organization.

Conformity Matrices

A conformity matrix helps to clearly show the difference between a standard-based approach and a process approach. (Take a glance at Figure 2 for an idea.) A conformity matrix describes how a company's QMS relates to the requirements of ISO 9001. Of course, a QMS is not designed to meet ISO 9001 requirements, it's designed to output quality product. A conformity matrix conveys how ISO 9001 requirements should be applied to a system, given the system's structure and design.

The requirements of the standard appear on the vertical axis of the matrix, while organizational processes are represented on the horizontal axis. Xs denote how the quality system addresses and conforms to the requirements, thereby indicating how the requirements apply to the organization's processes. Bear in mind that determining precisely where the Xs go requires an understanding of the organization's unique operations and how the organization has chosen to address each requirement.

If a solitary X appears on a row representing a requirement, the identified process addresses that requirement for the entire system. So some processes have system-wide application. Take Bob's Document Control process, for example. In Bob's case, document control provisions contained in the Document Control procedure pertain to all QMS documents. The standard's requirement for all QMS documents to be controlled is met with Bob's system-wide Document Control process.

Several Xs upon a row indicates that management appropriately addresses specific requirements in several processes. So, there are cases in which one process could effectively address requirements for the entire system, yet other cases where this isn't true. In Bob's case, the "product identification" requirements are addressed in the three processes where product is encountered: Receiving, Production, and Shipping. Understanding that some process and requirements have system-wide application and others don't, an auditor is supposed to determine (among other things) if management's defined arrangements are acceptable, i.e., effective.

So a conformity matrix is not an applicability matrix. An applicability matrix would place an X wherever the requirement is applicable— resulting in a page covered in Xs, which is hardly useful. For example, because the requirement to use controlled documents applies to any process using QMS documents, an auditor following an applicability matrix might ask a production worker how she controls the documents with which she works (because an X appears on the matrix where Production intersects with Document Control.) But it really isn't a production worker's job to control documents beyond protecting them. It's not her job, for example, to approve them, to apply revision control to them, or to control their distribution, etc. She just uses them. Following a conformity matrix, on the other hand, the auditor is focused upon activities most relevant to the process at hand.

If Bob's Machine Shop used a standard-based approach to achieve ISO 9002:1994 registration, it would result in the conformity matrix appearing in Figure 1 on the next page.

The Process Approach of ISO 9001

Figure 1

ISO 9000 Procedures			
A	4.1 Management Responsibility	J	4.11 Control of Inspection, Measuring and Test Equipment
B	4.2 Quality System	K	4.12 Inspection and Test Status
C	4.3 Contract Review	L	4.13 Control of Nonconforming Product
D	4.5 Document Control	M	4.14 Corrective and Preventive Action
E	4.6 Purchasing	N	4.15 Handling, Storage, Packaging, Preservation, and Delivery
F	4.7 Customer-Supplied Product	O	4.16 Quality Records
G	4.8 Product Identification and Traceability	P	4.17 Internal Quality Audits
H	4.9 Process Control	Q	4.18 Training
I	4.10 Inspection and Test	R	4.20 Statistical Techniques

ISO 9002:1994 elements	Description	A	B	C	D	E	F	G	H	I	J	K	L	M	N	O	P	Q	R
4.1	Management responsibility	X																	
4.2	Quality System		X																
4.3	Contract Review			X															
4.5	Document Control				X														
4.6	Purchasing					X													
4.7	Customer-supplied Product						X												
4.8	Product Identification and Traceability							X											
4.9	Process Control								X										
4.10	Inspection and Test									X									
4.11	Control of Inspection, Measuring and Test Equip.										X								
4.12	Inspection and Test Status											X							
4.13	Control of Nonconforming Product												X						
4.14	Corrective and Preventive Action													X					
4.15	Handling, Storage, Packaging, Preservation, and Delivery														X				
4.16	Quality Records															X			
4.17	Internal Quality Audits																X		
4.18	Training																	X	
4.20	Statistical Techniques																		X

The resulting eighteen documents are obviously designed to address the applicable elements of the standard. Notice how these documents hardly bear resemblance to organizational processes (i.e., Sales, Purchasing, Production, and Shipping and Receiving). Although often called procedures, they fail to address processes. This arrangement represents a perfect standard-based approach.

It sure looks orderly and straightforward. However, when using this approach, an organization making machined parts, a law office, and a day care service provider would all have the same procedural structure—despite their very different processes. Are these "procedures" helpful to management in managing processes? No. They don't begin to describe processes as processes. How do these "procedures" help employees understand company processes? They don't. Using a process approach, the ISO 9002:1994 matrix might look like Figure 2, below.

Figure 2

QMS Processes (and Procedures)			
A:	Sales	**E:**	Calibration
B:	Purchasing	**F:**	Training
C:	Shipping and Receiving	**G:**	Document and Record Control
D:	Production	**H:**	Internal Audits
		I:	Corrective and Preventive Action
		J:	Management Review

ISO 9002: 1994 elements	Description	A	B	C	D	E	F	G	H	I	J
4.1	Management responsibility										X
4.2	Quality System										X
4.3	Contract Review	X									
4.5	Document Control							X			
4.6-4.6.3	Purchasing		X								
4.6.4	Verification Purchased Product			X							
4.7	Customer-supplied Product			X	X						
4.8	Product ID and Traceability			X	X						
4.9	Process Control	X	X	X	X						
4.10	Inspection and Test			X	X						
4.11	Control of I, M & T Equipment					X					
4.12	Inspection and Test Status			X	X						
4.13	Control of NCP			X	X						
4.14	Corrective / Preventive Action									X	
4.15	Handling, S, P, P and Delivery			X	X						
4.16	Quality Records							X			
4.17	Internal Quality Audits								X		
4.18	Training						X				
4.20	Statistical Techniques			X	X						

The above ten procedures meet the applicable eighteen requirements in process fashion, meaning that the documents describe processes as they naturally occur. They describe these processes in such a way that conformity to applicable requirements is apparent. Notice how some requirements apply to more than one process, and some documents address more than one requirement.

Most important, notice how the procedures in the left column (A-D) reflect real organizational processes. They describe the operation and control of primary processes or core processes or—to use ISO 9000 parlance—realization processes. They also describe how these processes are managed in conformity with the standard's requirements.

The Process Approach of ISO 9001

Processes in the right-hand column of Figure 2 (processes E-J) are known as support processes. While realization processes are generally sequential, support processes typically operate in parallel with realization processes. As their name implies, these processes support realization processes to assure their effective and efficient operation. Taken together, realization and support processes compose a QMS, a system of processes. If one were to use a process approach with an ISO 9001:2008 matrix, it might look like Figure 3, below.

Figure 3

QMS Processes (and Procedures)													
A: Sales						**E:** Calibration							
B: Purchasing						**F:** Training							
C: Shipping and Receiving						**G:** Document and Record Control							
D: Production						**H:** Internal Audits							
						I: Corrective and Preventive Action							
						J: Management Review							

ISO 9001:2008 clauses	Description	A	B	C	D	E	F	G	H	I	J
4.1	General requirements										
4.2	Documentation requirements							X			
5	Management responsibility										X
6.1	Provision of resources										X
6.2	Human resources						X				
6.3/6.4	Infrastructure / W.E.										X
7.1	Planning product realization	X	X	X	X						X
7.2	Customer-related processes	X									
7.3	Design N/A										
7.4-7.4.2	Purchasing		X								
7.4.3	Verification of Purchased Product			X							
7.5.1	Production / service provision			X	X						
7.5.2	Validation of processes				X						
7.5.3	Identification / traceability			X	X						
7.5.4	Customer property			X	X						
7.5.5	Preservation of product			X	X						
7.6	Control of M & M devices					X					
8.2.1	Customer satisfaction	X									X
8.2.2	Internal audits								X		
8.2.3	M & M of processes										X
8.2.4	M & M of product			X	X						
8.3	Control of NCP			X	X						
8.4	Analysis of data										X
8.5.1	Improvement									X	X
8.5.2	Corrective action									X	
8.5.3	Preventive action									X	

[The general requirements of 4.1 do not appear on this matrix because they are addressed in the Quality Manual (as are many requirements at an upper level, in process fashion). Similarly, the exclusion of 7.3, Design, is also addressed in the Quality Manual.]

Figure 4

QMS Processes (and Procedures)		
A: Sales	**E:**	Calibration
B: Purchasing	**F:**	Training
C: Shipping and Receiving	**G:**	Document and Record Control
D: Production	**H:**	Internal Audits
	I:	Management Action
	J:	QMS Management

ISO 9001:2015 clauses	Description	A	B	C	D	E	F	G	H	I	J
4	Context of the organization										
5	Leadership										
6	Planning										
7.1	Resources (7.1.1-7.1.4, 7.1.6)										
7.1.5	Monitor/measuring resources					X					
7.2/7.3	Competence/Awareness						X				
7.4	Communication										
7.5	Documented information							X			
8.1	Operational planning/control	X	X	X	X						
8.2	Product/service. requirements	X									
8.3	Design/development (N/A)										
8.4	Purchasing/outsourcing		X								
8.5.1	Control of production/service	X	X	X	X						
8.5.2	Identification/ traceability			X	X						
8.5.3	External property	X		X	X						
8.5.4	Preservation			X	X						
8.5.5	Post-delivery activities	X		X	X						
8.5.6	Control of changes	X			X					X	
8.6	Release of products/services				X						
8.7	Nonconforming outputs		X	X	X						
9.1.1	General (9, Perf. eval.)										
9.1.2	Customer satisfaction	X									X
9.1.3	Analysis and evaluation										X
9.2	Internal audit								X		
9.3	Management review										X
10.1	General (10, Improvement)										X
10.2	Nonconformity/CA									X	
10.3	Continual improvement									X	X

The Process Approach of ISO 9001

Although a document called a "quality manual" isn't required of ISO 9001:2015, Bob chose to keep his manual. Not only does it satisfy customers requesting a quality manual, it maintains consistency with the sensible form of his existing system. Requirements shaded in the above matrix are addressed in Bob's quality manual.

Notice in Figures 2, 3 and 4 how the procedures and QMS structure remained the same despite the differences in arrangement between the 1987/1994, the 2000/2008, and the 2015 revisions of ISO 9001. Why? Because the processes and system structure didn't change significantly due to changes in the standard's structure. An organization's realization processes do not depend upon a standard. Rather, proper application of the standard depends upon an organization's processes and how an organization has chosen to define those processes. So using a process approach, a QMS is not re-defined for each new revision of the standard.

Notice also that process-based conformity matrices serve as valuable tools to an auditor applying a process approach to auditing. But that's a different story (which is briefly addressed later during a discussion of "Implications for Auditing," p. 141).

Sidetracked by a Standard-Based Approach
The twenty-element approach

What if we consider quality management without applying ISO 9001? QMSs exist independently of the standard, after all. Companies don't satisfy customers for years by accident, and many had been consistently satisfying customers long before ISO 9001 came along. But ISO 9001 did come along, and with it came unfamiliar requirements that were neither well understood nor well received by management.

By focusing solely on the technicalities of the requirements, businesses often lose sight of ISO 9001's real purpose. Ironically, a standard-based approach promotes poor quality management in the name of ISO 9001 certification.

Bob is the owner of Bob's Machine Shop, the contract manufacturer in our example. Bob's experience with ISO 9001 is not unlike that of other organizations. Bob's Machine Shop provides precision-machined parts to the manufacturing industry. Bob employs thirty people, most of them highly skilled machinists. Eighty percent of Bob's business relies upon a single original equipment manufacturer. The other twenty percent is a combination of smaller customers: twenty in all.

Bob is the General Manager of Bob's Machine Shop as well as its top salesperson and an important purchasing agent. Bob has three direct reports: the Sales Manager, the Purchasing Manager, and the Production Manager. The Production Manager also has three direct reports: two Production Supervisors and a Shipping and Receiving Supervisor.

Although Bob's Machine Shop has been in business since the 80s, it wasn't until the 90s that Bob's largest customer began requiring "ISO certification" of its suppliers. So, Bob began researching the options to achieve ISO certification. From all indications, the standard required lots of documented procedures. While books containing the required procedures were available, Bob decided to hire an ISO 9001 expert. He interviewed a few consultants and heard basically the same thing from all of them. He selected one.

The consultant explained that Bob's Machine Shop would be seeking certification to ISO 9002:1994. Bob's Machine Shop would need to adopt and implement a set of eighteen proven procedures—documents that had been used successfully for scores of other companies. The consultant assured Bob that each of these eighteen procedures represented the common-sense approach to demonstrate conformity to ISO 9002:1994.

Remember Bob's core processes affecting quality? The core processes are Sales, Purchasing, Receiving, Production, and Shipping. Bob understood that ISO 9002:1994 required eighteen procedures, but he was confused about how the following ten of the eighteen required procedures were supposed to help manage his five core processes:

- Contact review
- Purchasing
- Customer-supplied product
- Product identification and traceability
- Process control
- Inspection and testing
- Inspection and test status
- Control of nonconforming product
- Handling, storage, packaging, preservation and delivery
- Statistical techniques

Bob was understandably confused. Structuring QMSs in terms of the standard and documenting them accordingly results in standard-based documentation—obscuring processes rather than making them clear. They align perfectly with each requirement of the standard, but they have nothing to do with how Bob runs his business.

Figure 5 depicts Bob's five processes, contrasting the different documentation resulting from the standard-based approach and the process approach before the 2000 revision of the standard.

Figure 5

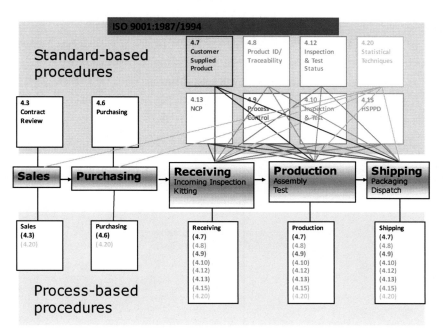

If a worker named Bill in the Receiving department was directed to receive a box according to the standard-based structure, he would have eight procedures to read—none of which tell him how to receive his box. Using the process approach, Bill has just one procedure to read and it tells him how to receive his box. By following a procedure that happens to meet all applicable requirements of the standard, Bill is also assured of complying with those requirements.

Notice the *Identification and traceability* requirements of ISO 9001 apply wherever product is encountered in processing. At Bob's, this requirement would apply to the Receiving process, the Production process, and the Shipping process, applying to several distinct activities within each process.

Using a process approach, QMS procedures bear a one-to-one correspondence with QMS processes—however management has decided to define them. One critical trick is to define processes at an appropriate level. Once a process is documented with a dedicated procedure, we can review it to determine if requirements applying to the process are adequately addressed. When processes fail to address requirements, sensible solutions are implemented and procedures are updated accordingly, as appropriate. When using the process approach to write a procedure, it's important to recognize how existing processing already meets requirements. This is a far cry from writing an armful of procedures to meet requirements first, then struggling to understand how to apply them to actual workflows.

Figure 6 contrasts Bob's processes defined using a standard-based approach and a process approach after release of the 2000 revision.

Figure 6

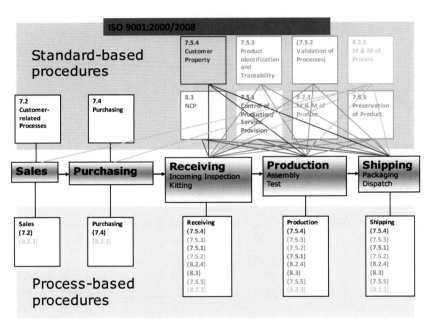

Notice that using a process approach, the basic structure of the system remains stable despite changes to the standard. Not owing its structure to ISO 9001, a process-based system provides a consistent basis for management through time. To meet future ISO 9001 requirements, a process-based system may simply need enhancements. It doesn't need to be re-defined to match each new revision of the standard. For organizations using a standard-based approach, it's never too soon to adopt the process approach.

There is no inherent conflict between ensuring conformity and assuring quality. The process approach addresses both efficiently and effectively, while the standard-based approach focuses on one—conformity—at the cost of the other. Under the standard-based approach, quality must endure despite a poorly-defined management system.

In summary, the 1987/1994 revisions of ISO 9001 did not require a separate documented procedure for each of the twenty elements. In Bob's case, ten procedures suffice to document his QMS (as management has defined it) in process approach fashion. The structure of these ten procedures stands up to the applicable elements of ISO 9002:1987/1994, as well as to the requirements of ISO 9001:2000/2008 and ISO 9001:2015.

The "Mandatory Six" Approach

The 2000 revision of ISO 9001 emerged with a reduced emphasis on documentation, as if responding to the voluminous, unwanted documentation produced by the standard-based approach under the 1987/1994 revisions. Under the 2000/2008, six procedures were often believed to be explicitly required. Under 2015, some believe no documented procedures are required at all to operate a management system.

Those promoting twenty procedures years ago seem to have been mistaken and those promoting only six procedures or no procedures seem equally mistaken. The problem with the twenty-procedure-standard-based approach was that despite the volume of documents, there could be no guarantee they addressed or defined the processes in need of management to assure quality. The problem with the mandatory six-procedure approach (or the no procedure approach) is the same: it fails to address or define the realization (or core) processes—the ones directly responsible for quality.

The Process Approach of ISO 9001

A natural response was to go from one extreme—often too many procedures—to the other extreme—too few procedures. Because the standard contains explicit requirements for only six procedures, it's easy to shirk documented procedures beyond the minimum required. While this might seem clever from a certification standpoint, it again fails from the perspective of sensible quality management.

The "mandatory six" procedures pertain to support processes or activities: internal audits, corrective action, preventive action, document control, record control, and nonconforming product. The standard requires procedural support of these processes (or activities). Does ISO 9001:2015 *require* documented? It would seem so, from the perspective of describing a quality management system. Further, they provide a foundation for effective assessment of a system. Some considerations:

Clause 4.4.1 of ISO 9001:2015 requires "The organization shall establish, implement, maintain and continually improve a quality management system, including the processes needed and their interactions. . ." 4.4.2 says, "To the extent necessary, the organization shall: a) maintain documented information to support the operation of its processes; b) retain documented information to have confidence that the process are being carried out as planned." "To the extent necessary," in my opinion, is not conveying permission to conclude the extent is "none," but to suggest that not all activities necessarily need to be supported by documented information. To be sure, the processes themselves needs to be supported by documented information (preferably by procedures describing how to properly carry out those processes).

It's a system of processes. Documented information must exist at an appropriate level to support operation of identified processes, documentation that is robust enough to assess whether or not processes are being performed according to procedure.

Clause 4.4.1 of ISO 9000:2015 requires organizations to determine the processes needed for the quality management system. If an organization operates procedures dedicated to requirements, in addition to or in place of procedures dedicated to QMS processes, that organization has failed to effectively determine processes needed for the QMS.

If operational processes have not been demonstrably determined (4.4.1) and documented (4.4.2), as required, an organization can hardly provide an acceptable description of the system and its processes, let alone their sequence and interaction. 20-element systems foisted non-processes into the description of the QMS and its processes; the "mandatory six" procedures failed to define realization processes in the first place.

8.1 e) requires documents, including records, determined by the organization to be necessary to ensure the effective planning, operation and control of its processes:

"determining, maintaining and retaining documented information to the extent necessary:
1) to have confidence that the processes have been carried out as planned;
2) to demonstrate the conformity of products and services to their requirements."

If no documented procedures exist, where are the documents ensuring the effective planning, operation and control of realization processes? If these documents exist, why not regard them as procedures?

Clause 8.5.1 of ISO 9001:2015 requires, as part of the controlled conditions under which production or service provision are supposed to be conducted:

"the availability of documented information that defines:
1) the characteristics of the products to be produced, the services to be provided, or the activities to be performed;
2) the results to be achieved . . ."

Did the 20-procedure approach or the "mandatory six" procedure approach demonstrate the effective planning, operation, and control of realization processes? No. Not in the least. This approach fails to define organizational processes, let alone the documents needed to ensure the effective planning, operation, and control of those processes. Of course the no procedure approach is unacceptable, too.

Here some might rebut with the following: "A blueprint and a router is all our employees need to make good parts. That's our procedure." This common argument demonstrates a focus on the sequence of activities directly responsible for product realization, e.g. a milling operation, followed by a turning operation, followed by a drilling operation. Sequences of activities like these are of utmost importance to quality.

Focusing only upon a sequence of activities representing where the rubber meets the road fails to recognize management activities needed to *define* the rubber and the road. When mistakes happen on the shop floor, many times it is due to errors made at a management level— problems that occur in management of the process. Management activities require control, just as shop floor activities do.

Process controls don't need to be painful. They just need to be well defined. For example, any reliable production process needs some level of production planning. Reliable quality doesn't happen by accident. A Production procedure should reasonably include or reference production planning.

- How do you know which parts/product to make?
- How do you know how many to make and when they are due?
- How do you know what product requirements exist and what acceptance criteria should be applied?
- Who determines the sequence of operations needed to realize product?
- Once set up, how many good ones can you expect to make in an hour?
- Who develops the Router and submits it to Production personnel?
- What resources are available to "production planners"?
- Who orders materials needed to make the product?
- Who procures order-specific tooling?
- Who establishes the shop scrap rate?

- Who posts the "On-Time-Delivery" chart and from where does the data come?

Here we are at the management level of the process—the level upon which the standard focuses. ISO 9001 is a standard for (quality) management systems (QMSs).

While of course QMSs must extend to shop floor activities, what should be under the scrutiny of an auditor is effective management of processes affecting quality and effective management of the system of processes. CB auditors will nevertheless examine processing details, but it's for the purpose of assessing effective implementation of the system.

Regarding realization or core processes, why in the world would one NOT define and document the most important processes of the system, pursuant to the PLAN phase of PDCA? A documented plan serves as a basis for the DCA phases of PDCA to work on. Sensibly documenting procedures benefits personnel expected to follow them, too. It also provides a benefit during audits. Leaving it undefined leaves personnel ad-libbing answers to auditors, or worse, it allows auditors to define your system for you.

Explaining it to Bob

ISO 9001 is a standard for effectiveness. The question is often, "Does it work?" Remember that it is important that the system works as defined.

What is a process?

Figure 7

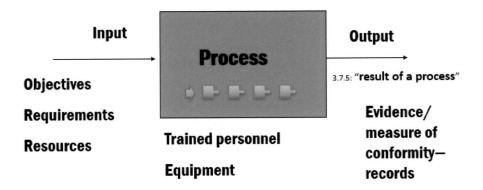

Process ISO 9000:2015, 3.4.1:

"set of interrelated or interacting activities that use inputs to deliver an intended result"

Preceding any controlled process is an objective. A process must accomplish something. Once we know what we intend to accomplish, the next step is to determine what activities are needed to accomplish it.

In Bob's Machine Shop, the Production process could be considered to begin when material and a Traveler is handed to a machinist. Travelers specify the sequences of machining activities needed to produce conforming parts. Travelers also call for quality inspections upon completion of first articles and prior to release to subsequent machining steps, thus it also serves as a quality plan using ISO 9000 parlance.

The objective of the Production process is to turn a piece of fairly nondescript metal into a precision-machined part meeting customer requirements within a defined tolerance (for example, five ten-thousandths of an inch). So the general process objective is to transform an input (raw material) into an output (a finished part). In addition to the process objective, other objectives are also established up front. Of course, one quality objective involves product conformity. Other quality objectives involve process effectiveness and efficiency.

Imagine that the blue arrow preceding the blue activities in Figure 7 represents the moment a machinist is handed raw material and its associated Traveler. The first activities might involve "setup." Here's one way the setup activities might be sequenced:

1. Verify the material against the Traveler.
2. Call up the CNC program to ensure all are in agreement.
3. Load tools into the machine per a setup sheet or instructions contained in the CNC computer.
4. Load the material into the machine.
5. Produce a first article (FA).
6. Obtain FA approval from QC.

Following setup, processing in production quantities would begin. Here, the expected output of the Production process is machined parts that have been verified to meet all applicable product requirements appearing on the blueprint.

With objectives clear and the sequence of activities clear, we can proceed with the DCA phases of PDCA. Figure 8 shows how PDCA is applied to a single process.

The Process Approach of ISO 9001

Figure 8

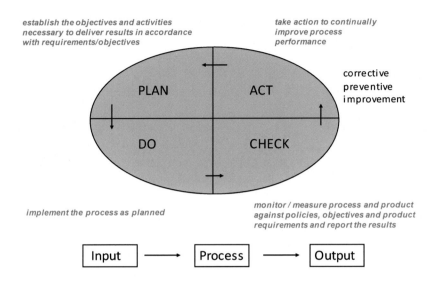

Once a process is defined, the PDCA cycle can be applied to improve its performance. Defining a process properly during the *plan* phase helps to promote consistent performance during the *do* phase. Businesses realize systemic process improvement by monitoring or measuring performance (*check*) and taking appropriate actions based upon resulting performance information (*act*).

Actions corrective in nature are taken when problems are detected during processing or during the *check* phase. Actions preventive in nature are taken to control recognized sources of error to preclude problems from occurring the first place. Improvement actions are taken not to address problems or potential problems, but simply to improve the process or product. Quality improvement in this regard involves reducing variation around a given target. For example, although the specified tolerance of five ten-thousandths was met last run, next run, we hope to more consistently achieve a product within three ten-thousandths of nominal. This improvement in product quality *results* from an improvement of the plan. Or, maybe a jig could be introduced to improve efficiency by reducing set-up time.

While a production plan might merely convey of a process how it to "get it done," a good QMS procedure conveys how to get it done properly, perhaps more focused on the goal of "getting it done well"— consistently, efficiently and with good results.

Quality, like quality management, is naturally built into any successful process. Managing quality, or managing anything it seems, involves application of PDCA. Systemic (quality) management involves applying PDCA at the activity, process, and system levels of a (quality) management system. So a linear production plan (see Figure 7) becomes an iterative cycle when we apply PDCA (Figure 8), to arrive at something below (Figure 9).

Figure 9

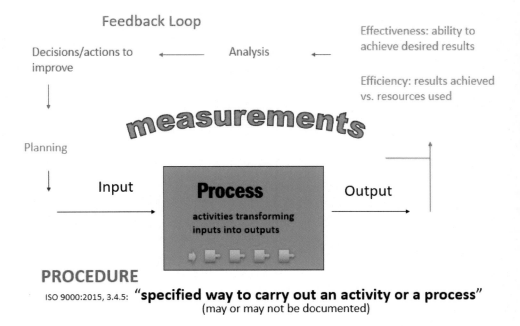

A procedure describes how a process is supposed to be performed. It represents the plan. It describes how a process flows, what activities are involved, and how those activities are controlled. Generally, Bob's plan for production, for example, is to output conforming product by following processing requirements appearing on Travelers. As mentioned previously, another result of process planning is established *performance objectives*. From a quality perspective, these would include process effectiveness (ability to produce conforming parts) and process efficiency (ability to achieve quality while expending as few resources as possible). An effective process results in outputs conforming to requirements. Process efficiency is a function of resources expended versus results achieved. Once performance objective are established, process performance will eventually be monitored or measured and evaluated accordingly.

According to Figure 8, measurements are applied before, during, and after processing. We check the inputs before we begin to ensure they are correct and consistent. During processing, we apply measurement, where appropriate, to ensure the process is functioning properly. We also measure product to ensure the process remains effective and to ensure the product conforms to applicable requirements for its processing stage. By monitoring processing and measuring product conformity, we can catch quality problems and remedy the situation before wasting additional resources. We can also use resulting performance information to improve, based on factual information about process performance relative to established processing objectives.

What is a (Quality Management) System?

A QMS might be defined as a system of interacting processes designed to output quality products. Using ISO 9000 terms, a QMS is composed of processes, while processes are composed of activities.

For example, applying a shipping label to a box could itself be considered a process. However, using the parlance of the standard, label application is one activity within the Shipping process. The "Shipping" procedure describes the sequence of shipping activities so they can be viewed, understood, and managed as part of one process: Shipping.

It's much easier to comply with, and demonstrate conformity to, procedures describing processes that happen every day: Sales, Purchasing, Receiving, Production, and Shipping. It's also much easier to insist personnel follow procedures. Otherwise, using a standard-based approach, management is stuck demonstrating conformity to unfamiliar procedures that do not make sense and that cannot be followed as processes.

Figure 10

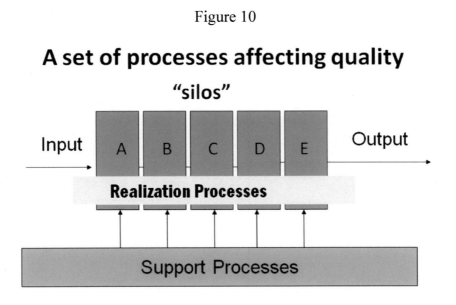

A set of processes affecting quality

adapted from ISO/TC 176/SC 2/N544R (May 2001)

While the diagram in Figure 10 (above) may depict a process approach, it fails to illustrate a system approach. The above set of processes could be managed in vacuums. It seems official guidance (ISO/TC 176/SC 2/N544R3) regards this as the "silo approach." That means the management of each process (perhaps viewed departmentally) might be concerned only about performance of its own process without regard to its impact upon other processes. In this situation, personnel responsible for executing individual processes are oblivious to overall system performance, customer satisfaction or profitability. A system approach basically amounts to applying the PDCA cycle to the system of processes itself, much the same way as the PDCA is applied to each process. Accordingly, system objectives are established, measurements of the system are applied, and performance is evaluated to improve the system and its processes.

The system approach meets the collection of processes:

Figure 11

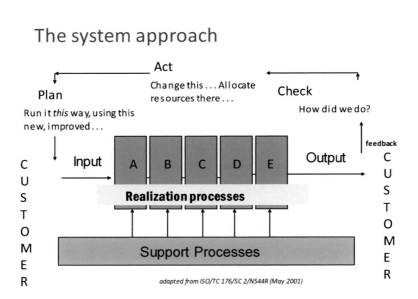

The system approach

Performance objectives at the process level are different from system level objectives. For example, set-up times, turn times, and reject rates might represent appropriate performance objectives for a Production process. They pertain only to production processing. Customer satisfaction and on-time delivery might be appropriate system objectives, as they pertain to the entire system of processes. Related measurements convey performance of the system of processes working together. To achieve on-time delivery, Sales personnel must agree to an attainable delivery date with the customer; Purchasing personnel must procure needed materials and tooling in a timely manner;

Production personnel must process the order in a timely manner; Shipping personnel must release product to assure timely delivery.

Implement a QMS, Not ISO

Saying that an organization is going to "implement ISO 9001" seems an imprecise use of terms. The word "implement" means "to put into effect." It seems more correct to state that a QMS is being implemented in an organization, one that may meet the requirements of ISO 9001.

When organizations say that they are implementing ISO 9001, they begin to turn to the standard to define their QMSs, often using a uniform structure designed to mirror the (uniform) requirements of ISO 9001 (e.g. today's common six-procedure structure, or yesteryear's 20-procedure structure). Of course, this has nothing to do with the actual purpose of ISO 9001—according to the standard itself. (See ISO 9001:2008, 0.1: "It is not the intent of this International Standard to imply uniformity in the structure of quality management systems or uniformity of documentation.")

While it's common for people to talk about ISO 9001 implementation, they are often talking about getting certified. This seems like putting the cart before the horse. The primary objective should be to sensibly define the QMS so it can be sensibly viewed and managed as a system of processes. Even if ISO certification is an objective, management should focus first upon the system that the standard is used to assess, rather than focusing first upon the assessment tool.

Roughly, ISO 9001 is for Auditors

This misunderstanding developed long ago. ISO 9001 is not an implementation tool. It's an assessment tool. Its purpose is to provide a uniform set of criteria against which QMSs are *assessed*. When ISO 9001 says, "The organization shall . . .", the standard (first party) is speaking to auditors (second party) about organizations (third party). The standard was written (for auditors, both internal and external) to be uniform criteria against which QMSs are assessed.

The Process Approach of ISO 9001

For years, organizations were told that ISO 9001 was addressing them directly. Thus, with the idea that the standard was addressing them, organizations got the idea that they were implementing ISO 9001 in their organizations. Then came the flood of uniform, standard-based QMS documentation.

Recognizing that organizations were misusing ISO 9001, ISO seemed to do two things in the 2000 revision. They admonished against the common standard-based approach while promoting a process approach in its stead. They also sought to make ISO 9001 more organization-friendly—partly to accommodate organizations that thought the standard directly addressed organizational management. (These organizations are customers, after all, so ISO showed some customer focus while also trying to convey proper use of the standard.) We can expect every future revision of ISO 9001 to endorse a process approach.

The same misunderstanding exists in requirements pertaining to top management. While some requirements pertain directly to top management, the standard is designed to talk to auditors about top management, not to directly address top management. Although the organization may be the subject of a sentence containing the words "the organization shall," organizational personnel are not the primary audience of the requirement. Management simply needs to comply with the requirements.

In ISO 9001:2000/2008, 0.1, the following was stated: "This International Standard can be used by internal and external parties, including certification bodies, to assess the organization's ability to meet customer, statutory and regulatory requirements applicable to the product, and the organization's own requirements." Nowhere did the standard say that it can or should be used by management to implement QMSs.

Conversely, look at the language of ISO 9004. When ISO 9001:2000 was released, it was released with ISO 9004:2000. They were promoted as being the "consistent pair." They complemented each other, going hand in hand. ISO 9001 contained requirements for assessing QMSs, using the word "shall" to denote requirements, while

ISO 9004 contained guidance for management, using the word "should."

ISO 9000 and 9004 represent the principles and guidance intended for management. However, to "get certified," management often went directly to ISO 9001, perhaps thinking it was the principles and guidance of the ISO 9000 series. Not recognizing ISO 9001 as a requirements document to which operations simply needed to conform, management often chose to define its QMS as being separate from operations.

That's why so many systems were raised by a clause-by-clause or six-procedure-only approach since release of the 2000 standard. Management went straight to the assessment tool to raise their QMSs. Instead, they should have gone to ISO 9000/9004 to understand the principles and for guidance for how to apply them when defining a QMS, and then used ISO 9001 to check the defined system for conformity to ISO 9001 requirements.

ISO 9000:2005, 0.1, General stated:

"ISO 9001 specifies requirements for a quality management system where an organization needs to demonstrate its ability to provide products that fulfill customer and applicable regulatory requirements and aims to enhance customer satisfaction."

If ISO 9001 was itself supposed to be implemented in organizations, it seems the above would be phrased something like, "ISO 9001 specifies the requirements for the design, structure, and implementation of a QMS," wouldn't it? Here's a phrase from ISO 900:2015, 0.1: "The potential benefits to an organization of implementing a quality management system based on this International Standard are . . ." Notice it's a *QMS* that is implemented. I wish this sentence said "conforming with" instead of "based on," because the idea of basing a QMS on ISO 9001 requirements invites use of a standard-based approach. (If a process approach is understood, however, this point is fairly mute.)

The Process Approach of ISO 9001

The standard specifies QMS requirements where an organization needs to demonstrate its ability to meet requirements. Of course, organizations demonstrate this ability every time good product is shipped to customers. However, because an organization satisfies its current customers at least well enough to stay in business, does it automatically follow that the organization would consistently meet requirements of new or potential customers? So organizations demonstrate their abilities to disinterested third-party auditors.

The language of ISO 9001:2015, 0.3, Process approach, also helps illustrate this point, although the clue is subtle. "Specific requirements *considered essential **to** the adoption of a process approach* are included in 4.4." (Italics and bold added.) Were this language intended for management of an organization, it seems the idea would be phrased, "essential *for adopting* the process approach." Stated that way, it would suggest the requirements are used for adopting the process approach, as if the requirements were intended to help organizational management implement a process approach.

It's not stated that way because these requirements are not supposed to be implemented by management. Management is supposed to implement a sensible QMS first, after which ISO 9001 requirements are applied. ISO 9001 provides auditors with criteria to determine if a process approach has been applied, given the provided requirements considered "essential to the adoption of a process approach."

So this language should not be taken to suggest that the requirements themselves are supposed to be implemented in organization. Instead, the requirements are specified to assess whether a process approach has been applied. In "specifying requirements essential to adopting a process approach," the intent isn't to tell organizations how to do it, but to ensure auditors can consistently assess whether it's been done.

What ISO 9001:2015 Says about the Process Approach
Introductory information about the process approach is found in ISO 9001:2015 at 0.3, Process approach—where it points us to 4.4 for the requirements. From ISO 9001:2015 4.4, "Quality management system and its processes":

4.4.1: "The organization shall establish, implement, maintain and continually improve a quality management system, including the processes needed and their interactions, in accordance with the requirements of this International Standard.

The organization shall determine the processes needed for the quality management system and their application throughout the organization, and shall:

a) determine the inputs required and the outputs expected from these processes;

b) determine the sequence and interaction of these processes;

    ..."

Comparing the requirements at the 4.4 of the ISO 9001:2015 to those at 4.1 of ISO 9001:2008, we find that the language of 2015 (4.4) very closely resembles the language of ISO 9001:2008 (4.4.1), with a few additions. One notable addition in 2015 (at 4.4a) is the requirement to determine process inputs and outputs. This should help auditors assess whether a defined QMS is effective, by analyzing whether inputs and outputs of processes reconcile to operate as a system outputting quality product.

Also, language at 0.1 of ISO 9001:2015, "General," mentions the process approach:

"This International Standard employs the process approach, which incorporates the Plan-Do-Check-Act (PDCA) cycle and risk-based thinking.

The process approach enables an organization to plan its processes and their interactions.

The PDCA cycle enables an organization to ensure that its processes are adequately resourced and managed, and that opportunities for improvement are determined and acted on . . ."

The Process Approach of ISO 9001

Why does the 2015 standard make the requirements to use a process approach more explicit?

One reason, it seems, is that many QMSs that fail to demonstrate a process approach still receive registration. Systems composed of standard-based documentation, for example, receive certification as quickly as those with properly designed and documented QMSs.

The application of ISO 9001 currently fails to discriminate between bona fide QMSs (resulting from a process approach) on the one hand and on the other, systems of documents (resulting from a standard-based approach). This fact tears at the very heart of the standard.

Section 5 of ISO 9001:2015 is headed "Leadership." 5.1, "Leadership and commitment," is followed by 5.1.1, "Leadership and commitment for the quality management system." At 5.1.1, we find the requirement: "Top management shall demonstrate leadership and commitment with respect to the quality management system by: . . ."

5.1.1a calls for top management to take accountability for the effectiveness of the QMS. If the QMS is not effective, top management is accountable for it. The responsibility for QMS effectiveness cannot be delegated to anyone. If a QMS is viewed as being a set of documents designed to pass audits, of course that can be delegated. But a set of documents isn't an effective QMS. A QMS is a system of processes keeping the organization in business. The effectiveness of a real system of processes cannot be delegated, say, to a Quality Manager.

5.1.1d calls for top management to ensure that the organization's QMS is integrated into business processes, as opposed to being defined according to the standard and then attached to business processes. As Deming suggested long ago, the standard now requires that quality be built into real organizational processes, rather than being viewed as something separate.

Also, 5.1.1e calls for top management to promote awareness of the process approach. The process approach is already naturally at work in any successful organization. The standard is making the process approach a priority for top management if certification is to be respected.

The Process Approach of ISO 9001

Procedures written in response to requirements do not effectively describe any process or system.

People talk about finding the "linkage" between the requirements. The only linkage should be a process itself. There is supposed to be linkage between activities of any given process, and linkage between processes of any given management system. The standard may apply to these linked processes and activities, but the standard itself does not provide this linkage.

Management can define processes however it makes sense (assuming a process approach). As long as planned arrangements are effective (the defined system outputs quality product), the CB auditor should be satisfied.

Here's one way to look at it: think of each realization process as a link on a chain. The chain begins with the acceptance of a customer order, and it culminates in delivering a quality product to the customer. (For now, imagine a straight length of chain, understanding that the actual arrangement of links in reality may be less linear.) Each link between the first and last is another process needed to realize quality product. Each plays a role without which the system could not function properly; the chain would be broken. How many links are needed? It depends upon an organization's purpose, how it is structured to operate, and how management chooses to define the links.

Think of upper-level processes in terms of process objective and functional role in the system. All of these processes have distinct objectives and serve distinct functions: Sales, Purchasing, Receiving, Production, and Shipping. Is Production one process? If management views it as such, then, yes. If there are several distinct production processes, notice none of them would likely be called "Production." In such a case, production might be broken down into Fabrication, Assembly, Paint and Installation. Each would be a link on the chain of core processes.

Together, the links of a chain represent a system of core processes. Depending on an organization's purpose, the first link might be Sales and Marketing, or it might be Design. It may end with Shipping or

Dispatch. Except for the very beginning, inputs to a system's process are outputs from other processes in the system. An effective arrangement defines these processes so that we can see how following this chain of events, tracing inputs to outputs, culminates in the timely release of quality product.

If effectively documented, it is clear how this chain of processes, each operating upon inputs and producing outputs, works together as a system. But what one organization might call a single process, e.g. Production—including CNC machining activities AND secondary operations—another organization might call two processes—Primary Operations and Secondary Operations. They can define it however they like, but best according to how they already view them, so long as the defined arrangement is effective.

Describe a process itself in terms of the controlled conditions under which activities or specific operations are performed. Describe how the process flows, specifying which activities are needed and how they are sequenced to operate upon process inputs to transform them into process outputs. QMS procedures are simply standard operating procedures (SOPs) with quality built into them. To draft an SOP, consider how operations are conducted today.

Is one fixed sequence of activities outputting the same product every day? If so, since the process apparently is designed to consistently output this one product, details of sequence can be included in the procedure.

In another scenario, if a process is expected to output unique product each time, the control over sequence might be established using a Traveler (or Router). A Traveler embodies the plan for how processing an individual order through a sequence of activities defined for processing that order. In a machine shop, a Traveler specifies the unique planning needed to achieve the process objective of the Production or Machining process (i.e., to output parts meeting print). It describes the sequence of milling and turning operations needed to transform raw material into a quality machined part. A Production procedure describing activity sequencing under this arrangement would do so with reference to a Traveler.

In yet another scenario, product may be realized in project fashion (perhaps involving the creation of new processes altogether). Project management often involves defining how a particular project will be planned and executed, orchestrating the unique coordination of several processes to achieve the desired results. Here, a project management function is often in place, as is a project management procedure (documented or not). Bear in mind that these procedures are followed every day to realize product.

In documenting procedures, we are describing management's plan for processing to be clear about the plan and how to implement it. Remember, good procedures describe processes pursuant to the plan phase of PDCA.

A process approach manifests itself differently in each organization.

To meet contractual requirements, a construction company may need to internally coordinate several departments (each dedicated to one or more processes): electrical, mechanical, fabrication, plumbing, etc.

In this case, a construction project is likely to be managed in project fashion. A Project Manager is often assigned to coordinate processes operated by various divisions, departments, functional units, or whatever they call them. "Process" in this sense might be viewed to flow between functions. In this case, the connection between departments or functional units is the Project Management process, a process unto itself.

Each department, division, unit, or whatever defined for the construction company operates at least one process. A procedure describing each process would describe the arrangements for performing activities of THAT process from the perspective of managing that process. A Project Management procedure would describe how a project is managed—including milestones, budget reporting, progress reports—to show how processes needed to assure quality are managed for each project.

In another case, say, a widget manufacturer making the same parts over and over, departmental processes likely will be performed the same way repeatedly in a more linear arrangement. In this case, while interaction with other processes is needed, each process is less subject to varying demands from other departments, unlike the construction company, where project-specific process interactions are wide and varied. Procedural provisions might adequately control process interaction in this production environment. Each order passing through production would not be treated in project fashion, so project management would not be needed as a process.

Just because the process approach can take many forms, it is important to remember that a standard-based approach is not one of them. A standard-based approach cannot demonstrate a process approach. As long as planned arrangements are effective, it doesn't matter how procedures are structured, but structuring procedures according to the uniform requirements of the standard is not acceptable. It will never result in effectively determining processes needed for a QMS.

Pre-Defined Quality Management

Quality management has become one-size-fits-all as the result of ISO 9001. The use of pre-written procedures to define QMSs is very common. It is a popular approach many have taken to achieve certification, and it encourages uniformity. The standard's authors never intended for quality management to be "canned" in the name of ISO 9001.

In the 1987/94 era, 20 procedures were said to be a good idea. Of course, when the same procedural structure is adopted by so many, QMSs all have the same basic format. Procedures were raised to uniformly address the requirements of the standard. While each organization is unique, many shared the same procedural structure, belying the uniqueness of quality management.

The Process Approach of ISO 9001

Under 2000/2008, with a minimum of six procedures ostensibly required, many elected to carry only six. Again, because of this, many organizations' defined QMSs did not reflect any organization's individuality—ignoring the (unique) realization processes that are the most important to any QMS. (By the way, it is more accurate to say that six clauses of the standard require documented procedures, than it is to say six procedures are required of the standard.) Procedures responding to requirements merely focus upon those aspects of processing addressed by the standard. None of them (even collectively) describe any business process. Such procedures are not scoped properly to describe how inputs are actually transformed into outputs during any given realization process.

The fact that the process approach is still so widely misunderstood and incorrectly applied more than a decade after the standard began demanding it suggests that ISO could have been more effective in clearly promoting this basic principle. But again, it seems less a problem with the standard itself, and more an issue with understanding and applying the process approach demanded by the standard.

The "One Big Process" Approach

Viewing several processes with distinct objectives as being one big process is not necessarily wrong, in fact, it is common among those in business to refer to their "process" as meaning either 1) what a user of ISO parlance would call a "system," or 2) a singular realization process fundamental to the organization's operation, a process without which it would have no product to sell in the first place. Again, these concepts of "process" are not completely incorrect, but they just weren't precise according to the technical use of the term per ISO 9000:2005.

One strategy to define QMS processes is to regard distinct processes involved with product realization (e.g. Sales, Purchasing, Receiving, Production, Shipping) as being sub-processes, all part of a larger "product realization" process or "demand fulfillment" process. When an organization defines "product realization" as being one big process, it seems we lose some useful granularity. It seems that a "product realization process" would actually be regarded in ISO parlance as a "system" of processes, this particular one scoped to describe only realization processes.

Instead of one big "product realization process" composed of "sub-processes," it seems these "sub-processes" (Sales, Purchasing, Receiving, Production, Shipping, etc.) are actually the processes needed by the organization to realize and deliver quality product. They are QMS processes, realization processes, business processes. These processes are the ones whose activities directly affect quality. Each has its own unique process objectives that align with those of the system of processes.

When Deming came upon the American manufacturing scene, "quality" basically meant one worker standing at the end of a production line sorting out the good from the bad. Deming suggested this was not very clever. When a part is scrapped by an end-of-line check, the organization has lost the time, labor, and materials it cost to make the scrap; the organization will spend time, labor and materials making a good replacement part, and if the first part were good, the organization would be making part number three (yet they are still stuck making part number one). Deming suggested moving quality checks and provisions into the processes, not waiting until the end. If we wait until the end, it's too late.

By definition, a process is a set of activities, not a set of sub-processes. Using the parlance of the standard, a system is composed of processes, each of which is composed of activities. "Sub-process" is not defined.

Inserting "sub-process" between "process" and "activity" seems to cause no conflict. The term "sub-process" seems acceptable so long as it doesn't conflict with the notion of "process" or "system" as the standard uses the terms. In other words, use of the term "sub-process" is okay so long as the "process" under which it is subsumed is viewed as being one process among a "system" of processes.

If, on the other hand, the term "sub-process" is evoked to allow for the definition of one big process (or even one big realization process)—conflicting with the notion of a system of processes—then it's a problem. Such a big process, it seems, is actually a system of processes, each with unique process objectives, each contributing to, and aligned with, system objectives.

The PDCA cycle can be applied to any activity, sub-process, or process, and also to a system of processes to improve performance at these various levels of organization. Notice the above model seems to fit with existing ISO definitions without introducing a concept not present in the standard: sub-processes.

Also, notice the standard (ISO 9001:2008, 4.1/ ISO 9001:2015, 4.4.1) calls for the processes needed for the system to be determined. The plural of "process" of course indicates more than one. As illustrated below, this distinction does not merely refer to the difference between realization/operational processes and support processes.

Per the standard, more than one realization process is also expected. Notice (2008, 7.1/ 2015, 8.1) that realization or operational requirements specifically call for processes. Again, the plural suggests that more than one realization or operational process is defined.

One process does not a system make. The plurality of processes implied by requirements pertaining to realization processes should also make clear that one realization process is also inadequate.

Risk and Quality

Now that risk is recognized (finally?) as being part of quality management—which is nothing new, risk is involved with every activity in life—some will likely knee-jerk react with an over-blown response to the inclusion of risk-based thinking among ISO 9001 requirements. To clearly comply with the requirement to apply risk-based thinking, some companies will no doubt be tempted to raise a "Risk Management" process and maybe even hire a "Risk Manager," even though neither is necessary to implement risk-based thinking or to comply with requirements to apply risk-based thinking.

Risk-Based Thinking

Risk-based thinking from a quality perspective is supposed to underlie management decisions affecting the (quality) management system, its processes, and the quality of its products, taking into consideration relevant interested parties (e.g., customers, end users, regulatory authorities). Sound business thinking (including quality management thinking), relies on risk-based thinking. Risk (to quality) must be assessed with an understanding of the organizational context: the industry in which the organization operates, the size of the organization, the education and skill level of organizational personnel, the impact of the organization's product on the world, etc.

Risk-based thinking is supposed to help assure any actions taken are appropriate to the risks involved. Understanding what is "appropriate" requires an understanding of the context giving rise to a risk issue. This includes understanding the issue in the context of the situation from which it arose, an understanding of the circumstances surrounding the issue. Like the requirements of ISO 9001 themselves, risk-based thinking cannot be applied in the abstract. It needs to be applied to an issue within a context. We often can't conclude what is risky and what isn't based merely on the identification of a risk issue. For example, what's a risky job for one organization (as product requirements approach capability limits) might not be risky at all for another organization (in which the requirements are well within normal operating parameters). So risk-based thinking necessarily requires the thinker to understand the context in which risk is being evaluated.

Risk-based thinking is a far cry from simply filling out a Preventive Action form with information enough to complete the form and consider the issue closed. Risk-based thinking encourages management to weigh the severity of a risk, its likelihood, and its potential consequences in the context giving rise to the situation.

Not every risk requires a 20-gun salute, but neither does every risk require to be effectively ignored. Actions to address any issue should take risk into consideration as a means of determining what is reasonable and prudent. It's along the line of ensuring actions are "commensurate with the risk encountered" (ISO 9001:1994, 4.14.1) or "appropriate to the effects of the potential problems" (ISO 9001:2008,

8.5.3)—meaning, the objective isn't to overkill (or under treat) any actions, but these actions should be appropriate, given the risk severity, likelihood, and potential consequences.

ISO 9001:2015, 6.1.1 says, "When planning for the quality management system, the organization shall consider the issues referred to in 4.1 and the requirements referred to in 4.2 and determine the risks and opportunities that need to be addressed to: a) give assurance that the quality management system can achieve its intended result(s); . . ." In other words, relevant risks are those that might impede the organizations ability to achieve intended results (e.g., resulting in the shipment of bad or late product).

So although the standard requires risk-based thinking, that doesn't mean a full blown risk management initiative for any organization seeking ISO 9001 registration. It means to take actions appropriate to the risk involved. Risk-based thinking deals with uncertainty, but it's nothing to be scared of. It's just prudent business thinking. While quality might urge us to do the right thing, risk-based thinking urges us to be smart about it.

How an ISO 9001 Project Proceeds

If you were new to ISO 9001 . . .

Get a copy current of ISO 9001. Also get a copy of ISO 9000 and ISO 9004. First read ISO 9000. When you get to the vocabulary section, pay attention to the definitions of "process" and "procedure."

Then pull out ISO 9001. Read it closely all the way up until you have completed the general requirements. Once you have read the general requirements, take your copies of ISO 9000, ISO 9001, and ISO 9004 and put them somewhere you can find them again in a month or few. (Otherwise, you might fall into the common pitfall of allowing the standard to define your QMS—a headache and a costly one at that.)

It's about YOUR (quality management) system first. Define it sensibly. Don't worry about the requirements at this point. It's already there; don't look to the standard or somebody else's documentation to develop your own system documentation. Nobody does what you do like you do. Define it for yourself.

Here's one way to get started:

Determine processes needed for the system. The system is composed of processes, and each process is composed of activities. Processes needed for the system are upper level processes—management processes. Processes affecting quality are basically those whose activities bear upon product/service conformity/quality.

In a smaller manufacturing company, there might be only a few processes. For example, you might have a Sales-type process, a Purchasing process, a Manufacturing process, and a Receiving and Shipping process. In a larger organization, manufacturing processing might consist of separate divisions or departments—say, Fabrication, Assembly, and Paint. The main point is to pay attention to the existing organizational structure.

Once you have defined your processes, a good idea is to document them sensibly, taking into consideration your existing process documentation. If a procedure that describes the process from inputs to outputs already exists, great. If not, writing one isn't difficult.

Create a template so that all of the processes will be described consistently. (Not required, just a nice touch.) You can use text documents, flow charts, process flows, turtle diagrams, etc. It's helpful if a procedure states what the process objectives are, upon what inputs the process operates, and what outputs it produces. Of course, a section dedicated to describing the process is important. Templates can always be adjusted once you see what works in practice. It seems short text documents work best to describe processing, while at the same time conveying internal processing requirements and being clear about how ISO 9001 requirements are met.

The Process Approach of ISO 9001

To write a procedure, understand that the people managing and performing the process are the process experts. Ask them. Ask how and where it starts, how the process flows, and what controls are in place to ensure proper processing. Draft a procedure using the template, based upon information provided by your own process experts. When you are finished, ask them to review it. Make adjustments until everyone agrees. Now you have a process-based procedure.

Move to the next process and repeat. Make sure inputs and outputs match up. Once you have your current business processes documented sensibly, you will have defined the "realization" processes of your QMS. Good job. Now you can retrieve your copy of ISO 9001. Read it carefully and notice how your system documentation satisfies (or fails to satisfy) the requirements.

At this point you are ready for a gap analysis. You may notice that your system doesn't address requirements for, say, internal auditing. Maybe you don't have defined controls pertaining to document control, corrective action, or calibration. You might get help with developing these controls. You might even use someone else's procedures to define an internal audit process. But this is appropriate only in the case of these support processes or activities. Never use somebody else's procedures to define the most important processes of your system: the primary, core, realization, operational-type processes. These processes, by definition, are unique to your business. They are the intellectual property that creates your competitive advantage.

Since you are already certified . . .

If we assume Bob's Machine was certified to the 1994 revision of the standard and maintained a standard-based QMS structure up until now, I would advise Bob to do the following:

Bob would eliminate nine procedures and replace them with two. Gone would be "Quality System," "Customer Property," "Product Identification and Traceability," "Process Control," "Inspection and Test," "Inspection and Test Status," "Preservation of Product," "Control of Nonconforming Product," and "Statistical Techniques."

However, Bob might use some of the provisions in these procedures to draft process-based procedures, so his team would need to be careful not to eliminate valuable information while rewriting.

Bob would have to bear in mind that these are requirements of a standard for assessing systems—actually, a mix of 1994 and 2000/2008 requirements, as was common. They are not QMS processes. If, for the sake of argument, we consider the above requirements as being QMS processes, remember that the standard requires monitoring and improvement of QMS processes. How does one monitor and improve, say, the "Customer Property" process? Or the "Inspection and Test Status" process? Or the "Product Identification and Traceability" process?

How much effort should be expended in improving performance of these processes? None. They are not and never were processes—at least not in most organizations.

To dedicate a QMS procedure to each requirement is to assert a QMS process for each requirement. According to ISO 9000:2015, 3.4.5, a procedure is defined as a "specified way to carry out an activity or a process . . ." So if you have a procedure, you have a process (or an activity). A procedure conveys the right way to carry it out. If there were no right way, then there would be no procedure.

Again, a QMS procedure implies a QMS process. QMS procedures specify how processes needed for the management system are carried out. A process, per ISO 9000:2015, 3.4.1, is defined as a "set of interrelated or interacting activities that use inputs to deliver an intended result." It's something that happens, something that operates upon inputs and transforms them into outputs.

To employ a process approach to documenting a QMS, Bob needs to align his QMS procedures with his own QMS processes. He would start by replacing the nine trashed "procedures" with two sensible ones: "Production" and "Shipping and Receiving." While shipping is a separate process from receiving, in Bob's case both processes are performed in the same area, by the same personnel, and in what Bob has defined as the "Shipping and Receiving" department. That's why it doesn't hurt to combine the procedures in one document to reflect the organizational structure. Since storage of incoming and finished goods falls under the responsibilities of this department, it makes sense to include a section dedicated to storage within the "Shipping and Receiving" procedure. Bob doesn't need to describe storage as a separate QMS process. It is effectively addressed as part of the "Shipping and Receiving" procedure.

Also, include appropriate provisions within the "Shipping and Receiving" procedure and within the "Production" procedure describing the respective routines for identifying, evaluating, and managing the disposition of nonconforming product. You will notice that the conformity matrices in Figures 3 and 4 already reflect this suggestion.

Once these procedures are drafted, review them to ensure they address applicable requirements at an appropriate level to capture how conformity is achieved. Edit procedures to be clear how requirements are met. That way, it's clear to everyone how processing meets requirements. In a sense, you are interpreting the standard to your organization. If a process does not meet the applicable requirements, implement sensible solutions. Use the procedure to help implement these solutions, if necessary.

Process interaction at Bob's

Figure 12 depicts a detailed, yet upper-level view of process interactions between Bob's business processes: Sales, Purchasing, Receiving, Production, and Shipping.

Figure 12

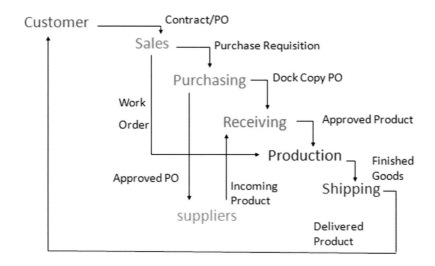

Sales

Above, a customer submits a contract to the organization. It is received via the Sales process and further processed according to the Sales procedure. Accordingly, upon order acceptance, a purchase requisition to procure materials and services needed to fulfill the order's requirements are submitted to the Purchasing department for processing according to the Purchasing procedure. These constitute inputs to the Purchasing process. Another output of the Sales process is a work order, which constitutes an input to the Production process (specifically, the production planning part of the process).

Purchasing

Operating upon the above input, outputs of the Purchasing process are purchase orders specifying materials and services needed to fulfill contractual requirements. Purchase orders are submitted to suppliers for fulfillment. Copies of placed purchase orders are also considered outputs of this process. These are submitted to the Receiving department and will eventually serve as acceptance criteria, pertaining to incoming purchased goods and services according to the Receiving procedure.

Receiving

When incoming goods and services arrive from suppliers, Receiving personnel verify their acceptability in part based upon requirements appearing on copies of placed purchase orders (from Purchasing, above). Once personnel have verified incoming product, they approve it for use in Production and release it for use.

Production

Production of each work order is planned and executed according to priorities established during production planning. Based upon product information and due dates appearing on accepted Work Orders, Travelers are developed and released according to the Production procedure. Using approved Travelers and materials approved for use by incoming inspection, orders are processed and finished product is output. Finished product is destined for the Shipping department.

Shipping

Given the handling, packaging, and shipping requirements appearing on Travelers accompanying finished product to Shipping, Shipping personnel use appropriate packaging materials to protect product during shipment. Product packaged for shipment is labeled and released to customers according to their preferred method (also specified on Travelers).

These processes work together every day to output quality product. Good QMS documentation describes these processes and how they work together to output quality product and satisfy customers.

General overview of process-based QMS documentation

The following depicts a typical documentation structure. The manual describes a system of processes. A (QMS) procedure describes each process, often referencing use of third level documentation. (Notice nowhere does this model suggest that processes should be defined according to the standard's requirements.)

Figure 13

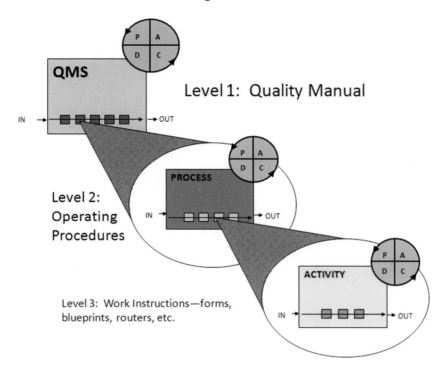

The PDCA cycle can be applied at every level of QMS structure, the definition of which is reflected by process-based QMS documentation. Bear in mind that not every detail of every process or activity needs to be documented for it to be effectively communicated. Personnel can be trained to know details, too.

To be clear, ISO 900:2015 doesn't require a document titled "quality manual." The above documentation structure isn't required. Particularly in smaller companies, it might make sense to capture all system-level documented information (levels one and two) into one document. That document could be called a "Quality Manual," an "Operations Manual," or simply, "It" for that matter.

The Process Approach Meets Bob's Machine Shop

An overview of a QMS per official guidance suggests that in reality, QMSs are not as linear as previously depicted.

Figure 14

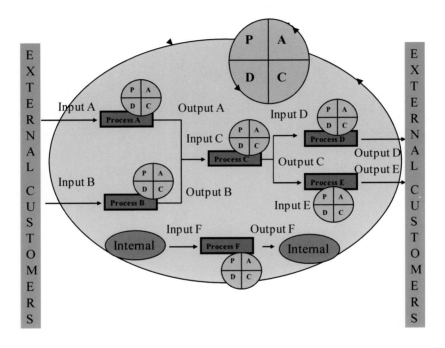

(Adapted from ISO/TC 176/SC 2/N544R, May 2001)

Refer back to figure 12—quality begins and ends with the customer. The customer has needs expressed in the form of requirements, and seeks a supplier to satisfy those requirements. Once a suitable supplier has been found, the customer stops seeking a supplier and purchases the promised product or service. At this point, the customer expects to be satisfied, meaning that the supplier will deliver on the promise, and that the supplied product or service will meet requirements. In other words, the customer expects quality.

Figure 14 depicts several processes, or departments' *operating* processes, within a given QMS. Notice that some of the processes (A through E) transform inputs into outputs that are eventually offered to the customer. Another process, F, begins and ends internally. Processes A through E are regarded as realization processes because they represent the critical path to quality product/service delivery.

On the other hand, Process F, while part of the QMS, is not critical path to delivery. It is a support process. The customers of its outputs are internal and are not intended for an external customer. Notice how the Deming cycle, PDCA, can be applied to the QMS as a whole and to each of the processes comprising the system.

For example, perhaps a company needs ball bearings. It develops specifications or requirements for the bearings—requirements that must be met to ensure the suitability of the bearings for their intended use. The company searches for a supplier who is in the business of producing ball bearings meeting the defined requirements. Once a suitable supplier is found, one who pledges to meet the requirements, the company issues a purchase order.

From the perspective of the company that buys ball bearings, the supplier might be viewed as a process (a process that outputs ball bearings). The supplier organization might be viewed as being a button on a vending machine. The customer specifies a product, presses a button, and expects ball bearings that meet the specified requirements to drop out.

When product is delivered, the customer has some level of satisfaction. If the supplied product meets all applicable requirements, then the customer should be reasonably satisfied. If the product failed to meet applicable requirements, the customer may reasonably be dissatisfied. If the product is better than the customer expected, the customer may be delighted.

A diagram offered in ISO 9001:2008, 0.2, Process approach, "Model of a process-based quality management system" illustrates an organization's system for satisfying customers (and now "interested parties"). This same model is applicable to each process in a QMS, as well as to the QMS as a whole:

Figure 15

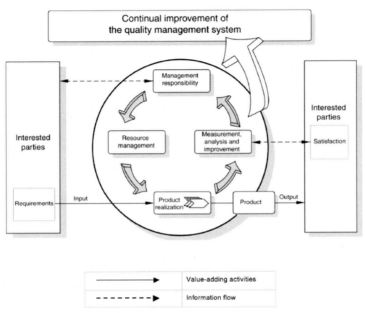

Figure 1 — Model of a process-based quality management system

Working left to right, the flow of the diagram begins with the customer, more specifically, with customer requirements. These requirements constitute an input to a supplier's QMS. In this case, the supplier is the organization responsible for meeting customer requirements.

Looking at the circle representing a QMS in Figure 15, notice four distinct pieces in it (again working left to right, following the arrows):

Resource management

Product realization

Measurement, analysis and improvement

Management responsibility

These four pieces correlate to the major clauses of ISO 9001:2000, clauses 6, 7, 8, and 5, respectively. The QMS, like the documentation describing it, is addressed by the general requirements of clause 4.

Notice an input to the left of the circle and an output (product) to the right. Between the input and the output is a circle that represents a QMS—a process (or, a *system* of processes) transforming inputs into outputs.

The four pieces within the circle are not necessarily actual processes within an organization. Rather, they are all parts of a systemic method of managing organizational processes—a method of managing the QMS and its processes toward improvement.

In Figure 6, customer requirements enter the QMS where the input line intersects the circle. At this point, assume the customer has provided requirements and the organization has promised to meet those requirements.

Before proceeding, take a step back and look at this circle. What do you see? Preferred answer: *the Deming cycle*—the plan-do-check-act cycle.

From ISO 9001:2008, 0.2 (the text immediately preceding their Figure 1):

"The model of a process-based quality management system shown in Figure 1 [appearing as Figure 15 in this book] illustrates the process linkages presented in clauses 4 – 8. This illustration shows that customers play a significant role in defining requirements as inputs. Monitoring of customer satisfaction requires the evaluation of information relating to customer perception as to whether the organization has met customer requirements. The model shown in Figure 1 [my Figure 15] covers all the requirements of this International Standard but does not show processes at a detailed level.

The Process Approach of ISO 9001

Note: In addition, the methodology known as 'Plan-Do-Check-Act' (PDCA) can be applied to all processes. PDCA can be briefly described as follows:

Plan: Establish the objectives and processes necessary to deliver results in accordance with customer requirements and the organization's policies.

Do: Implement the plan.

Check: Monitor and measure processes and product against policies, objectives, and requirements for the product and report results.

Act: Take actions to continually improve process performance."

ISO 90011:2015, Figure 2 [my Figure 16, below], offers another depiction of how PDCA relates to the clause structure of the standard:

Figure 16

0.3.2 Plan-Do-Check-Act cycle The PDCA cycle can be applied to all processes and to the quality management system as a whole. Figure 2 illustrates how Clauses 4 to 10 can be grouped in relation to the PDCA cycle.

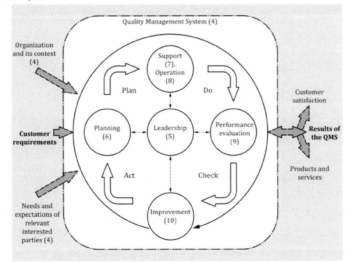

NOTE Numbers in brackets refer to the clauses in this International Standard.

Figure 2 — Representation of the structure of this International Standard in the PDCA cycle

Put Deming in Your QMS

PLAN. In my Figure 15, "Resource management" represents planning. Resources are subsumed under section 7 in the 2015 standard (my Figure 16], the result of planning. Planning needs to consider resource requirements for support processes, just as they do for realization processes.

Management of an existing organization has acquired and organized resources, including human resources and infrastructure resources (e.g. buildings, processing equipment, tools, process documentation, etc.), to operate primary processes in an orderly manner and realize saleable products or services. These resources are arranged in their current configuration, which was the result of some type of planning—good or bad, formal or informal, systemic or otherwise. At any rate, resource management represents the current plan for processing orders through the arranged resources to output quality products. The current configuration of resources results from the *plan* phase of the Deming cycle.

DO. Upon reception of input requirements from the customer, an organization's processes operate to output product (or service) that will satisfy the customer. Processes directly involved with producing finished product are called *product realization* or *operational* or *primary* processes. Such processes have a direct impact on fulfilling customers' requirements. These are the primary processes of the organization, processes necessary for quality product delivery, processes necessary for the organization to survive.

As an example to illustrate realization processes, consider a ball bearing supplier's QMS as including a *sales* process: a process through which customer requirements are determined and the company's ability to meet those requirements is verified. Without this process, quality product delivery could not be expected with any degree of confidence. Sales, therefore, is a realization process. Another realization process might be *purchasing*, where the appropriate raw bar stock is purchased, bar stock that will eventually be received through a *receiving* process, transformed into ball bearings during *production*, and released to customers by a *shipping* process. All are realization processes, as the business cannot operate without any one of them.

Product realization processes, or departments operating those processes, are those directly necessary to produce the product or service intended for the customer. The objectives of these processes directly involve transforming inputs into outputs that are intended for an external customer.

Given input requirements from a customer, an organization's process, or system of processes, transforms *something* into product (or service) that meets those requirements. In Figure 15, notice the product being output from the organization's system, on its way to the customer. *Product realization* represents the *do* phase of the Deming cycle.

CHECK. "Measurement, analysis, and improvement" represents not only the measurement applied to product to ensure its conformity, but also the measurement applied to processes to ensure their control (as the large arrow in Figure 15 signifies). It also represents the customer's perception of the organization's performance, signified by the dotted line extending from "satisfaction" into a QMS's function for collecting and analyzing such measurement/monitoring data. The results of analysis identify where improvements to the system and its processes can be made. *Measurement, analysis, and improvement* represents the *check* phase of the Deming cycle.

ACT. Management is responsible for making improvements whenever it is deemed necessary to ensure conformity of product, improve the product or service relative to customer requirements, or improve the effectiveness or efficiency of the system and its processes. Ideally, improvements should be made based upon factual information from the *check* phase, and should result in adjustments to the planned arrangements and associated resources. Of course, improvements are also made as a result of reports of nonconforming product or other undesirable circumstances. Improvements might include additions to the infrastructure or modifications to it, training personnel, or modifying documentation. Effective actions change *something*, even if it's as simple as adding a check box to a form to prevent someone from overlooking a step in the future. Such a slight change still affects the resources available to personnel whose work impacts quality. *Management responsibility* represents the *act* phase of the Deming cycle.

Once properly applied to a process or system of processes, the Deming cycle helps drive improvement. One key to ISO 9001 is understanding the process approach. In a sense, ISO 9001 presupposes the process approach, as does the Deming cycle itself in the context of QMSs. A QMS should be viewed and managed as a system of processes affecting quality. Without the process approach, management will struggle to properly view, measure, and manage the processes affecting quality. That is no doubt in part why ISO 9001:2000 explicitly endorsed the process approach. If a plan is good and customers are satisfied, management might choose not to drastically change it. Why fix what isn't broken? But there is room for improvement in any organization, especially in a world where customer requirements are constantly changing. What works today might not work in the future. So, as the world changes, organizations must change along with it to survive, sometimes significantly. It is management's responsibility to continually improve the organization (i.e., increase its ability to fulfill requirements) in order to remain competitive in an ever-changing world.

Those hoping ISO 9001 would improve their businesses for them were given false hopes; it is, and always will be, managements' job to improve their organizations, processes, and systems. As stated earlier, ISO 9001 is for auditors, not for managers.

By viewing and managing a QMS as a system of processes, management has adopted the process/systems approach to quality management. In order to set the stage for continual process evolution, management must do three things. It is necessary to establish objectives for quality, to measure performance in relation to those objectives, and to manage processes to achieve those objectives. In this way, management is managing the system and its processes toward improvement. Through a routine cycle of planning, doing, checking, and taking actions to improve, the Deming cycle improves the QMS and its processes.

The Process Approach of ISO 9001

Paul Batalden, M.D., professor at The Dartmouth Institute for Health Policy and Clinical Practice, tells us:

"Every system is perfectly designed to get the results it gets." [http://www.dartmouth.edu/~cecs/hcild/hcild.html]

Phrased slightly differently using ISO 9001 parlance, "Every system is perfectly designed for its outputs."

This idea seems applicable to all kinds of systems designed by human beings, including management systems. For one example, if a system is performing at ninety-two percent by some measure, then that system is in a sense designed to succeed ninety-two percent of the time. It's therefore also effectively designed to fail eight percent of the time. So an opportunity for improvement exists.

While numeric data and controls have their place in managing operations and in improving performance, effective management often involves knowing when and where to apply them. Deming taught us to eliminate quotas in order to establish or improve performance of the workforce at an operations level. He also sought to eliminate using numbers in certain ways at the management level.

In his book, *Out of the Crisis*, Deming lists his famous 14 points. At point 11.b (p. 24), Deming tells us: "Eliminate management by objective." and "Eliminate management by numbers, numerical goals. Substitute leadership."

A process or system might be considered stable when some measurement of performance consistently operates within established parameters (or at, say, ninety-two percent). This baseline performance level provides a foundation for improvement. To achieve improvement, some will choose a management by objective strategy, using specific numeric performance targets established somewhat arbitrarily, at least somewhere above the current baseline performance level. Then management does what it can to achieve this objective, including demanding of everyone that the "improved" objective must be achieved.

Remember, every system is perfectly designed for its output. System measures convey, in a sense, the level at which system is designed to perform. Again, a system succeeding ninety-two percent of the time is effectively designed to succeed ninety-two percent of the time. Management is not likely to improve performance by simply declaring an objective of ninety-three percent or better and insisting that this improvement happens somehow.

Deming seems to suggest management by objective fosters conditions ripe for adversarial relationships, while also inviting perceptions of failure. Rather than setting an arbitrary, numeric objective up front, based on current performance, and then expecting a system to perform better than it was effectively designed to perform, presumably via sheer willpower or "by gosh and by golly," Deming suggests substituting this numeric management game with leadership.

Make improvements to the system at every level of operations and encourage improvement at every level of operations. If performance is to improve, the system needs to be improved. With purposeful application of PDCA to various aspects of operations, improvements will yield better performance results. Performance measures reflecting improved performance then provide evidence of improvement, while also providing a foundation for any further improvement. Numeric data and statistical controls appropriate for applying PDCA in certain operations, control points, or circumstances are not appropriate at the management level when it comes to driving performance improvement. Though a statistician, Deming seemed to recognize limitations to the value numbers offer management.

As Figure 15 illustrates with the large arrow extending from the top of the circle, diligent application of PDCA results in continual improvement of the QMS, improvement that may be extended to the organization as a whole.

Process/System Approach, Meet Bob's Machine Shop

Bob's quality manual contains a diagram showing the sequence and interaction of Bob's QMS processes. (See Figure 17.) Process interaction is more specifically addressed in QMS procedures. While the diagram might appear busy at first, it's less intimidating once broken down.

Customer requirements (solid black line) enter Bob's QMS (on the left) via the Sales process. Once accepted, product and delivery requirements are forwarded to Production for production planning. Product and delivery requirements are also communicated to the Purchasing department for procurement of materials, outsourced processes, and/or other resource requirements.

The Purchasing department submits POs to suppliers to procure the needed materials, services, or other resources. Copies of placed POs are also sent to the Shipping and Receiving department, against which incoming goods will be verified during receiving. Incoming goods (dotted gold line) enter the system via the Receiving process. Accepted goods are staged for use in Production. Once production planning is complete and Travelers have been generated, Production personnel manufacture product according to Travelers, using materials dedicated to the order.

Finished product (solid gold line) is submitted to Shipping for packaging and transport to the customer. Once the customer receives the finished product, Sales personnel elicit feedback (via the customer communications routine described in the Sales procedure). This performance information (blue line) is provided to Management Review; performance information from each QMS process is also provided to Management Review.

Each QMS process requires resources. At Bob's Machine Shop, resource requirements are satisfied by a centralized Purchasing process. Resource requirements arise from each QMS process, some more than others.

Figure 17

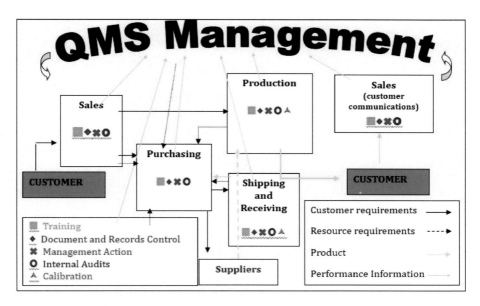

The block in the lower left corner contains icons representing support processes. Situated within the core processes, the icons depict which core processes the support processes support. For example, the Document Control and Training processes support all other processes; Calibration only sits in support of the Receiving and Production processes (the only processes in which calibrated devices are used). Support processes also support each other, as appropriate.

This QMS overview diagram defines each process in the system so that together they can be viewed and managed as a system of processes. The Deming cycle can be applied to each process, to activities within each process, and to the system as a whole. Though the same PDCA model can be applied to a process and to a system of processes, objectives are different at each level. Stated or otherwise, objectives exist at the activity level, the process level, and the system level. Objectives must precede any controlled process.

Quality objectives generally consist of goals for effectiveness and goals for efficiency. Effectiveness measures often include assessments of resulting product to determine product conformity; effectiveness measures reveal whether or not the process is working (i.e., producing conforming product) and the degree to which it is under control (i.e., reliable or consistent performance). Efficiency measures, on the other hand, involve assessments of results achieved juxtaposed against resources consumed in processing. These are more directed at process improvement (i.e., reducing variation around a given target, or increasing capability or capacity, or achieving higher levels of performance related to established performance levels).

Process objectives and measures are different from system objectives and measures. For example, in Bob's situation, objectives and measurements of the sales process involve order entry accuracy. Those for the purchasing process involve production down time due to late material arrival, whereas those for production include set-up times, turn times, and reject rates. These are examples of *process* objectives and measures—they pertain only to their respective processes.

On the other hand, system objectives and measures involve customer satisfaction, for example, or on time delivery. These objectives and measures reflect the ability of the QMS processes to work together as a *system*.

Bob's Realization Processes (and Procedures)

Caveat: the following procedures are provided as examples only—they are not for cut-and-paste purposes. Adopting someone else's documented procedures will always pinch you in the end.

To document Bob's five realization processes—Sales, Purchasing, Receiving, Production, and Shipping—we would write four procedures because Shipping and Receiving are combined in one procedure. Because the Shipping and Receiving processes both operate in the Shipping and Receiving department, the departmental procedure addresses both processes. It is one document containing two procedures. (Or, it could be viewed as one procedure addressing two sequences of activities.)

We basically took the processes in order, anticipating procedures between three and five pages in length. Understanding that more detail can (and likely will) be added as necessary in the future, we opted to keep the procedures fairly general. In the future, adding more detail might be driven by an effort to improve the process or to correct processing deficiencies, for example. Having a documented procedure in place provides a framework to help communicate new processing requirements, so they can help implement corrections and improvements.

Because Bob's personnel are generally well trained and experienced, and because existing process documentation (e.g. paper and electronic forms) has proven effective, highly detailed procedural guidance was deemed unnecessary in this instance.

However, Bob mentioned that the highest turnover rate arose from the Shipping and Receiving department—specifically Receiving. Although departmental personnel are cross-trained to perform both processes, the Receiving folks do most of the receiving and material check-in, while the Shipping folks do most of the packaging and release. Three of Bob's current machinists started in Receiving. We decided to add a little more detail to the Receiving procedure to help reinforce instructions provided during training.

The Process Approach of ISO 9001

Because Bob's Machine Shop does not operate special processes, the requirements of ISO 9001:2008, 7.5.2 (Validation of processes) do not pertain to the Production process and are not addressed in the Production procedure. (Controls pertaining to providers of special processes are addressed in the Purchasing and Receiving procedures, however.)

By format, these procedures will address process objectives, responsibilities, and inputs and outputs. The heart of the procedure describes the sequences of activities composing the process, as well as any existing controls in place to ensure quality in processing. Each procedure naturally mentions the controls in place to assure activities are performed properly and resulting product meets requirements.

Sales

Because Bob knew the Sales process, he provided all the information needed to describe the process. Because the process is fairly short and simple, the procedure reflects that. According to the ISO 9001:2015 conformity matrix (Figure 4), activities of the sales process needed to comply with the requirements of 8.2 (Requirements for products and services) and 9.1.2 (customer satisfaction). As a realization process, it must also be planned per 8.5.1.

Here's what we came up with:

SALES   Rev. D

1. Objectives and Purpose

1.1. Objectives

1.1.1. <u>Process objective</u>: Aligning with the system objectives of customer satisfaction, quality product release, and on time delivery, an objective of the Sales process is to ensure our ability to keep our promises. This specifically includes assessing capability for providing product conforming to specified product requirements, and for assessing capacity to meet established delivery dates. Another objective of the Sales process involves effective production planning, including generation of Travelers used in Production.

1.1.2. <u>Performance objectives</u>: It is a primary objective of the Sales process to maintain a high capacity utilization and a consistent volume of workflow. More specific performance objectives are established, measured, and tracked as prescribed during Management Review. (See the QMS Management procedure.)

1.1.3. Generally, the purpose of this procedure is to ensure that Sales activities are performed under controlled conditions. This procedure describes specific arrangements for developing and submitting quotations, and for processing purchase orders from customers—including Traveler development and order changes. This procedure also describes arrangements for communicating with customers regarding product information, complaints, feedback, customer satisfaction, and order handling.

2. Responsibility and Applicability

2.1. This procedure is applicable to all sales activities conducted at Bob's Machine Shop, as well as to personnel performing sales activities.

2.2. Sales personnel are responsible for maintaining relationships with customers, responding to customer inquiries, providing product information, developing and submitting quotations, receiving, reviewing and accepting orders from customers, and responding to customers' requests to change accepted orders.

2.3. The President is responsible for ensuring that this procedure is accurate, understood and implemented effectively. This procedure may not be changed without the authorization of the President.

The Process Approach of ISO 9001

3. Inputs and Outputs

3.1. Inputs to the Sales process include product, pricing, and availability information, inquiries (e.g. regarding pricing and availability), RFQs, and POs from customers, which include product and delivery requirements. Change requests and feedback (including complaints and satisfaction information) also constitute inputs to the Sales process

3.2. Outputs of the Sales process include quotations that are offered to customers, accepted POs from customers and records associated with the above activities. Outputs also include Travelers and job lists for use in Production, as well as product information for use in Purchasing. Finally, outputs also include customer communication records and completed customer satisfaction surveys.

4. Procedure

4.1. General

4.1.1. Sales personnel perform processing activities according to documented work instructions (e.g. posted work aids, flow charts, etc.) and according to instructions to which they have been trained. (See the Training procedure.)

4.1.2. Sales personnel identify the need to purchase resources needed for operation of the Sales process. These are brought to the attention of the Sales Manager. If identified items are confirmed to be needed, they are procured according to the Purchasing procedure. (The need to procure materials, services, or other resources specific to the processing of any given order is fulfilled based upon Manufacturing Requirements Planning (MRP) data associated with accepted customer orders, as described in the following procedure.)

4.1.3. Documents used during processing are controlled according to the Document and Record Control procedure (and this procedure), as are records generated during processing.

4.2. Product Information, Inquiries and Customer Communications

4.2.1. Management reviews and approves product information and process capability information before it is published in the public domain (e.g. in brochures, flyers, or on the web site).

4.2.2. Sales personnel answer inquiries regarding pricing and availability to the best of their ability according to current pricing and production demand. Sales personnel are authorized to distribute approved product literature.

4.2.3. When customers contact Bob's Machine Shop regarding the status of their order, Sales personnel determine order status and respond to customers accordingly. To determine order status, Sales personnel may consult Production Management or refer to data in the MRP system.

4.2.4. When customers contact the company with feedback, suggestions, complaints, or returns, such communications are addressed according to section 4.5 of this procedure.

Requests for Quotations (RFQs) and Quotations

4.2.5. Sales personnel determine whether to pursue customer RFQs depending on whether or not they represent a good business opportunity and whether or not the requested products fall within the current capabilities of Bob's Machine Shop. (Rejected RFQs may be discarded.)

4.2.6. Sales personnel ensure the appropriate information is on hand, including part number and revision of requested products, their quantities, and due dates.

4.2.7. Requested products are verified to fall within Bob's Machine Shop's current processing and verification capabilities. Sales personnel consult with the Production Manager as necessary to identify any tooling or other materials required to process orders, and to suggest routings. (The Production Manager may also suggest no-quotes.)

4.2.8. As necessary to determine adequate capacity, Sales personnel determine current production demand by consulting Production Management, and/or by researching production demand information in the MRP system.

4.2.9. Sales personnel develop quotations using the MRP system. Quotations are developed to capture relevant customer requirements, including any multiple release requirements. Quotes also include planned production operations necessary to realize product, including estimates of materials and labor, and outsourced processing.

4.2.10. Completed quotations are reviewed to ensure they are correct and can be met before being submitted to customers. (Disapproved quotations are corrected and reviewed again.) Only approved quotes are released. Evidence of approval also resides on each electronic quotation itself. Records of approved quotations are maintained in the MRP system. After 30 days, orders are re-quoted at the discretion of Sales personnel.

4.3. Purchase Orders from Customers

4.3.1. Purchase Orders from customers must be received in writing. When an incoming PO refers to an existing quotation, the quotation is reviewed against its corresponding PO to ensure consistency between the two. Any discrepancies are resolved before proceeding. If no quotation is available, Sales personnel develop one as described earlier before proceeding, unless the order represents a repeat order. Repeat orders are re-quoted at the discretion of Sales personnel.

4.3.2. Customer POs are reviewed to ensure customers' requirements are clear, including product requirements, delivery dates, and any additional requirements, such as certification or traceability requirements, inspection requirements, special handling requirements, packaging or shipping requirements, etc., as applicable. If ambiguities exist, the customer is contacted for clarification, as necessary. This review also ensures that Bob's Machine Shop has the ability to meet customer requirements. As necessary, production demand is determined (as described earlier for quotations), and the likely lead time to meet customer orders is evaluated. Should the estimated actual ship date required differ from the requested due date, the customer is notified and approval is obtained before proceeding, as required.

4.3.3. An electronic Sales Order is generated in the MRP system for each PO meeting the above requirements. Saving a Sales Order to the system is evidence of its approval. Order acknowledgements are sent to customers, as required. Any hard-copy drawings remain with their orders in the Open Orders file pending release to Production.

4.4. Traveler Generation

4.4.1. Repeat orders

> 4.4.1.1. Using the MRP system, Sales personnel access part number history files to verify part numbers and revision levels of incoming orders match those on file before proceeding.

> 4.4.1.2. Once verified that the requested part numbers and revisions levels are one file, Sales personnel generate Travelers for accepted orders.

4.4.2. New orders

> 4.4.2.1. Orders for which there is no part number history are new orders. Product information gathered during the quotation phase is used to develop Travelers, as are routings of similar parts.

> 4.4.2.2. The Production Manager and the Quality Manager are consulted as necessary to assist with new Traveler

development. (Before release for use in Production, Travelers require approval of the Production Manager and the Quality Manager pursuant to the Production procedure.)

4.4.2.3. Any special customer requirements are recorded on Travelers ("notes"), including critical dimensions, special handling or packaging, etc. Upon successful review and approval, Travelers are saved in the MRP system ("pending approval") according to job numbers. (See the Production procedure.)

4.4.3. Sales personnel generate job lists on a weekly basis. Job lists are developed using data from the MRP system and production availability/demand information from the Production Manager. Job lists establish priorities for production. (See the Production procedure.)

4.4.4. Upon completion of production and shipping, Travelers of closed orders are returned to Sales personnel for storage in the closed Travelers file. Associated hard-copy drawings are disposed of. If quantities are still owed, Travelers are submitted to Preproduction personnel, who re-schedule due quantities in the MRP system. Any updates required of Travelers are made electronically, reviewed, and approved as described previously, after which closed Travelers are filed in the closed Traveler files.

4.5. Order Changes

4.5.1. When customers contact Bob's Machine Shop to change an accepted order, Sales personnel review the nature of the changes against the original order, and react appropriately, including locating the product and stopping processing, if appropriate. Should change orders be received verbally, they are confirmed before proceeding. Written change orders are requested, as are any updated specifications or other requirements.

4.5.2. Change orders are reviewed and approved in the same manner as new orders (above).

4.5.2.1. If requested changes are simple and can be accommodated (e.g. order quantities or due dates), Sales personnel locate the associated traveler package and amend the Traveler accordingly. Such amendments are initialed and dated to indicate approval.

4.5.2.2. If a requested change is more complex (e.g. dimensional changes), a modified PO and updated drawings/specifications are required before proceeding. Such orders are re-quoted as described earlier at the discretion of Sales personnel. Sales personnel may revise customer blueprints as directed by customers while awaiting updated documentation. Such revisions are initialed and dated to indicate approval.

4.5.3. Upon approval, change orders are communicated to Production Management personnel via new or updated Travelers and drawings.

4.5.4. If the requested changes cannot be accommodated, the customer is notified for resolution and a new agreement may be developed, reviewed, and approved as a new order, or else the order may be refused.

4.6. Customer Feedback

4.6.1. When customers contact Bob's Machine Shop with information regarding performance (e.g. product quality, delivery, or general performance), complaints, or suggestions for improvement, such communications are routed to Sales personnel. Such communications are recorded in the electronic Customer Communications log.

4.6.2. Customer communications are reviewed to determine if action is required. If action is required, a Management Action may be initiated according to the Management Action procedure. Management contacts customers, as appropriate, to inform them of any actions taken to address their concerns, while records of such communications are maintained in the log.

4.6.3. If a complaint involves returning product, Sales personnel arrange for the return using the Returned Material Authorization (RMA) routine in MRP. Accordingly, Sales personnel create RMAs, recording job number, part number and revision, and reason for return. Comments include a description of the problem, the date rejected, and the original packing list number. Packing lists are electronically reopened, the parts are un-shipped, and the order is returned to open orders (in MRP). Returned product is evaluated by QC and dispositioned according to the nonconforming product routine described in the Production procedure. MRP records reflect final disposition.

4.7. Customer Satisfaction

4.7.1. Customer surveys are conducted on an annual basis using satisfaction surveys. The results of each such survey are recorded on survey forms. (Customers who routinely supply us with satisfaction information do not require surveys. In such cases, customer satisfaction is determined using the customer-supplied information.) Sales personnel review results as they become available and react appropriately according to the information received, initiating Action Forms as appropriate.

4.7.2. Customer satisfaction is determined based upon performance indicators including quality, delivery, returns, customer communications, and survey results. Such information is submitted to top management during Management Review. (See the QMS Management procedure.)

4.8. Change History

4.8.1. Original issue: 09/13/95

4.8.2. Generally re-written to meet requirements of ISO 9001:2000: 09/15/00

4.8.3. Re-titled and generally re-written to describe the Sales process (complying with ISO 9001): 09/17/13

Purchasing

The Purchasing Manager was available to define the purchasing process. At Bob's Machine Shop, it is viewed as a centralized process, meaning that if somebody needed something, they went to purchasing to get it.

According to the conformity matrix, activities of the Purchasing process are responsible for demonstrating conformity to requirements appearing in ISO 9001:2015, 8.4 (8.4.1-8.4.3). Per the matrix, dispositioning nonconforming product (8.7) is also part of the Purchasing process. Again, since Purchasing is considered a production or operational process, 8.5.1 applies, too.

Here's what we came up with:

PURCHASING   Rev. B

1. Objectives and Purpose

1.1. Objectives

1.1.1. Process objective: Aligning with the system objectives of customer satisfaction, quality product release, and on time delivery, the Purchasing process assures the quality of products and services representing inputs to our processing as well as their timely delivery. The objective of the Purchasing process is to procure goods and services needed to fulfill customer orders, as well as those needed to operate and support processes needed to produce goods and services offered to customers. A related objective of the Purchasing process is to ensure suppliers of goods and services dependably provide quality goods and services.

1.1.2. Performance objectives: A primary objective of the Purchasing process to ensure resource needs are fulfilled in a timely manner, and are consistently made available when and where needed. More specific performance objectives are established, measured, and tracked as prescribed during Management Review. (See the QMS Management procedure.)

1.2. The purpose of this procedure is to describe the purchasing functions, including the evaluation, selection and re-evaluation of suppliers, as well as the review and approval of purchasing information to insure that it describes needed products and services in the requisite detail before their transmission.

2. Responsibility and Applicability

2.1. This procedure applies to purchased products and services that affect the quality of Bob's Machine Shop's products and processes. This procedure is applicable to Purchasing personnel, who are involved with purchasing and the evaluation and approval of suppliers.

2.2. The President is responsible for ensuring that this procedure is accurate, understood and implemented effectively. No changes may be made to this procedure without the authorization of the President.

3. Inputs and Outputs

3.1. Inputs to the Purchasing process include information for specific products appearing on accepted POs from customers. Inputs also include including those for outsourced processing (e.g. finishing, machining, special processing, etc.), operating supplies, and supporting services (e.g. utilities, shipping carriers, etc.).

3.2. Outputs of the Purchasing process include supplier approval records, approved Purchase Orders, and purchased products and services meeting purchasing requirements.

4. Procedure

4.1. General

4.1.1. Purchasing personnel perform processing activities according to documented work instructions (e.g. posted work aids, flow charts, etc.) and according to instructions on which they have been trained. (See the Training procedure.)

4.1.2. Purchasing personnel identify the need to purchase resources needed for operation of the Purchasing process. These are brought to the attention of the Purchasing Manager. If identified items are confirmed to be needed, they are procured according to this procedure.

4.1.3. Documents used during processing are controlled according to the Document and Record Control procedure (and this procedure), as are records generated during processing.

4.2. Supplier Evaluation, Approval and Re-evaluation

4.2.1. Bob's Machine Shop uses approved suppliers to fulfill Purchase Orders for goods or services affecting quality, except in cases when a supplier is being evaluated or when a product or service is urgently needed. (Records of such purchases will be maintained in order to evaluate supplier performance and to consider supplier approval.)

4.2.2. Suppliers appear in an electronic list within the Manufacturing Requirements Planning (MRP) system. Approved suppliers appear with an "active" status. Disapproved suppliers appear with an "inactive" status.

4.2.3. Purchasing personnel evaluate and select potential suppliers (i.e., those who have never supplied products or services in the past). Such suppliers are evaluated before routine use to ensure their ability to supply product in accordance with purchasing requirements, and in consideration of their impact on processing and final product quality.

Selection depends upon a supplier's ability to meet purchasing requirements, based on references, information provided by the supplier, and/or by using the supplier on a probationary basis.

4.2.4. Suppliers of special processes (i.e., considered to be process resulting in outputs that cannot be verified by inspection or testing methods available in-house) are further qualified as required of customers. Internally, the ability to provide accredited certificates supporting claims of conformity is verified. (See "special process qualification" remarks for suppliers of special processes in the suppliers' module of the MRP system.)

4.2.5. Suppliers are continually re-evaluated with the receipt of each product supplied. When suppliers provide untimely or discrepant products or services, the nature of the discrepancy will be recorded on associated packing lists, which are retained in the Supplier Incident file (available via the MRP system). Purchasing personnel resolve any such issues, submitting corrective actions to offending suppliers, as appropriate.

4.2.6. Approved suppliers retain their status at the discretion of the Purchasing personnel. Status changes are based upon supplier performance (e.g. supplier incidents, including quality and delivery performance, and/or corrective actions issued), as well as pricing or availability issues. Purchasing personnel may, at any time, decide that poor performance by the above criteria warrants a change to a supplier's approval status.

4.2.7. Suppliers are also periodically re-evaluated during Management Review meetings, where the President and meeting attendees examine the contents of (or summaries of) any supplier incidents, performance information, and/or corrective actions issued to suppliers to determine their continued acceptability. Records of this evaluation are maintained in Management Review minutes, while any resulting status changes are reflected in the electronic suppliers list.

4.3. Purchasing

4.3.1. Any employee may identify the need to purchase goods and services to support, operate, or improve processes affecting quality.

4.3.1.1. The need to purchase raw materials, tooling, outsourced processing, etc., associated with a particular customer order is identified by Sales personnel during the Sales process. These are available to Purchasing personnel via the MRP system.

4.3.1.2. Resource requirements needed to operate processes or to improve process effectiveness or efficiency may be identified by anyone in the company. These are brought to the attention of management (see the associated procedures), who fulfill resource needs by communicating them to Purchasing personnel. Purchasing requirements are communicated via purchase requisitions, which must bear approval of management personnel.

4.3.1.3. Purchase requisitions may take a variety of forms (e.g. requisitions made via the MRP system, formal or informal paper requisitions, or emails). To be clear, the Sales Manager, Purchasing Manager, Production Manager, Production Supervisors, and the Quality Manager are authorized to submit purchase requisitions, as is the General Manager.

4.3.1.4. Based in part upon input from management, the General Manager ultimately determines whether or not to proceed with capital expenditures—significant additions or modifications to the infrastructure or work environment—including additions or modifications to work areas and the facility as a whole. (See the QMS Management procedure.)

4.3.2. To procure needed items or services, Purchasing personnel complete Purchase Orders (POs) using the PO module of the MRP system. Purchasing personnel review the written purchasing requirements to ensure they are accurate and complete, including, as appropriate:

4.3.2.1. Product information qualifying and quantifying the needed product or service in adequate detail to ensure relevant requirements are communicated properly to suppliers. Product requirements may be included in, or represented by, part numbers or other specifications. Such requirements may include: product type, grade, dimensions and tolerances, quantities, revision levels, catalogue numbers, finish or color requirements, etc., as well as make, model, etc. Such requirements may also include shipping/delivery requirements, and, as appropriate, further criteria for acceptability of the product or service (e.g. traceability, certifications of conformance, etc.), as required.

4.3.2.2. Delivery requirements (including any lead-time requirements).

4.3.2.3. Any requirements relating to acceptability or approval of suppliers' processes are added to purchase orders, including: including the qualification of the equipment, procedures, and/or personnel performing work affecting quality, as well as any requirements for quality management systems. Such requirements may include reference to industry standards, quality standards, (e.g. ISO 9001), certifications of qualifications for equipment or personnel, special processing, etc.

4.3.3. POs meeting the above requirements are considered approved, evidenced by an "approved" check box upon the electronic PO. If certificates are required of raw material or calibrated devices, Purchasing personnel verify such requirements to be stated on associated POs before approval. Evidence of PO approval resides on each PO itself, also with an indication of the requesting approval authority (via initials).

4.3.4. Purchasing personnel transmit approved POs to suppliers. Purchasing personnel may place POs verbally over the telephone, in which case suppliers are requested to read back the requirements to ensure they were fully communicated. Written POs always follow verbal orders. Copies of placed orders are kept in the Receiving area pending receipt. (See the Shipping and Receiving procedure.)

4.3.5. Incoming product is verified according to the Shipping and Receiving procedure. Purchasing personnel disposition any nonconforming product discovered during receiving inspections. Disposition (e.g. return to supplier) is recorded on associated packing lists, while product is processed accordingly. Records of such incidents are retained in the Supplier Incidents file.

4.3.6. Upon successful incoming verification, POs are placed in the Closed PO files and are closed electronically in the MRP system.

4.4. Order Changes and Cancellations

4.4.1. When purchasing requirements change (or are cancelled) for any reason Purchasing personnel may make the necessary changes to the original POs in the MRP system.

4.4.2. Revised POs are reviewed, approved, and printed in the same manner as new POs, while the MRP system automatically prints a new approval date on changed POs. Approved, updated POs are sent to the recipients of the originals. Suppliers are also verbally notified of changed orders, as appropriate. (If a supplier cannot accommodate the changes, Purchasing personnel will resolve the issue, which may involve renegotiating an agreement, or requesting quotations from other suppliers.)

4.5. Verification at Suppliers' Premises

4.5.1. If Bob's Machine Shop or our customers want to verify product at our suppliers' premises, such requirements will be included in the associated Purchase Orders. Purchasing personnel will make arrangements accordingly.

4.6. Change History

4.6.1. Original issue: 09/13/95

4.6.2. Generally re-written to meet requirements of ISO 9001:2000: 09/15/00

4.6.3. Generally re-written to describe the Purchasing process (complying with ISO 9001): 09/17/13

Shipping and Receiving

The following seven requirements of ISO 9001:2015 pertain to the Shipping and Receiving processes (per the matrix in Figure 4) and are to be addressed and met by the "Shipping and Receiving" procedure:

8.1, Operational planning and control,

8.5.1, Control of production and service provision,

8.5.2, Identification and traceability,

8.5.3, Property belonging to customers or external providers,

8.5.4, Preservation,

8.5.5, Post-delivery activities, and

8.7, Nonconforming outputs.

After interviewing Bob, the General Manager, and Shipping and Receiving personnel of Bob's Machine Shop, we came up with a "Shipping and Receiving" procedure, below.

For demonstration purposes (since this is the first process where actual product is encountered), clause numbers of applicable ISO 9001:2015 requirements appear in brackets beside clauses within section four in the procedure. These are a non-comprehensive suggestion for how procedural provisions address requirements. While addressed at an appropriate level for the activities described, some requirements are fully met by reference to other procedures.

Of course, requirements for personnel to be trained, for documents and records to be controlled, and for calibrated devices to be used in measuring product conformity also apply to shipping and receiving activities. While these are addressed appropriately by this procedure, the primary focus is on the above seven requirements.

SHIPPING AND RECEIVING   Rev C

1. Objective and Purpose

1.1. Objectives

1.1.1. Process objectives: Aligning with the system objectives of customer satisfaction, quality product release, and on time delivery, the primary objective of the Receiving process is to receive and verify incoming goods to ensure they meet purchasing requirements. Another objective of the Receiving process is to store accepted materials and purchased items, preserving their conformity pending use in production. The primary objective of the Shipping process is to properly package and release products according to customer requirements. Another objective of the Shipping process is to store finished goods in inventory, preserving their conformity pending future release to customers.

1.1.2. Performance objectives: A primary objective of the Receiving process is to consistently ensure the quality and timeliness of incoming goods and services before their acceptance and release for internal use. A primary objective of the Shipping process is to consistently ensure the quality of packaging and effective product preservation, as well as to ensure shipping documentation accuracy. More specific performance objectives are established, measured, and tracked as prescribed during Management Review. (See the QMS Management procedure.)

1.2. The purpose of this procedure is to describe the Receiving process, including the verification and storage of purchased product and customer property. This procedure also describes the Shipping process, including verification, packaging, and release of product to customers. This procedure also addresses handling, packaging and preservation, product identification, and control of nonconforming product.

2. Responsibility and Applicability

2.1. This procedure is applicable to all Shipping and Receiving personnel, who are responsible for receiving, verifying, packaging, storing and releasing product, and also to Purchasing and Quality Control (QC) personnel, who are responsible for inspecting and/or dispositioning nonconforming product discovered during processing. This procedure applies to all incoming products and services that affect the quality of company products and processes.

2.2. The General Manager is responsible for ensuring that this procedure is accurate, understood, and implemented effectively. No changes may be made to this procedure without the authorization of the General Manager.

3. Inputs and Outputs

3.1. Inputs to the Receiving process include copies of Purchase Orders (POs) and their associated Travelers, as appropriate (which contain or reference acceptance criteria against which incoming product is verified/inspected), incoming products (or supplied services), packing lists which accompany incoming product, as well as any supporting documentation such as material or process certifications. Customer property and product returning from customers also constitute inputs to the Receiving process. Inputs to the Shipping process include product destined for outsourced processing, finished product, and requirements to release product to customers or to finished goods inventory (FGI).

3.2. Outputs of the Receiving process include accepted product and evidence of verification, which includes signed packing lists, electronic data, and QC inspection reports. Nonconforming product is occasionally an output of the Receiving process, as are the records of its disposition and records of supplier incidents. (See the Purchasing procedure.) Outputs of the Shipping process include product released to customers according to their requirements and records of release (e.g. completed Travelers).

4. Procedure

4.1. General

4.1.1. Shipping and Receiving personnel perform departmental activities according to documented work instructions (e.g. posted work aids, flow charts, Travelers, etc.) and according to instructions to which they have been trained. (See the Training procedure.) [(7.2, 7.3) 8.1, 8.5.1a,g,e]

4.1.2. Shipping and Receiving personnel identify the need to purchase packaging and shipping supplies as stock levels of these items become depleted along with other resources needed for the operation of the Shipping and Receiving process. These are brought to the attention of Production Supervisors or the Production Manager. Once the identified items are confirmed to be needed, they are procured according to the Purchasing procedure. [8.1, 8.5.1h]

4.1.3. Documents used during processing are controlled according to the Document and Record Control procedure (and this procedure), as are records generated during processing. [(7.5) 8.1, 8.5.1a]

4.1.4. Personnel who are required to use calibrated devices are trained in their selection, handling, and use to ensure continued accuracy of measurements and continued fitness of the instruments. Any devices used to demonstrate conformity of product during receiving are controlled according to the Calibration procedure. [(7.2, 7.1.5) 8.1, 8.5.1b,e]

4.1.5. Employees handle and store items carefully to ensure their own safety and the safety of others. All employees involved in product handling and storage do so to preserve product conformity and to maintain product identification. Appropriate handling methods and transport equipment are used at all times. [8.1, 8.5.1a,d, 8.5.2, 8.5.4]

4.1.6. Incoming goods are identified by accompanying packing lists (or equivalents). Incoming product may also be identified by its physical appearance, by accompanying documents (e.g. certificates), as well as by part numbers and/or labeling on the product or its packaging. Travelers further identify incoming materials that are dedicated to particular orders. Travelers also identify requirements for QC inspections and/or material traceability, as applicable. [8.1, 8.5.1a, 8.5.2]

4.1.7. Incoming customer property (e.g. material or tooling) is further identified by customer name, job number, and/or part number. Should customers supply measuring devices, they are submitted to QC personnel. (See the Calibration procedure.) Customer property is handled, used/processed, stored and preserved in the same manner as purchased product. Should customer property become lost or damaged, it is brought to the attention of the General Manager. Such incidents are recorded in the customer communication log and customers are notified via email. Management action is initiated, as appropriate, and customers are informed of any actions taken to resolve problems and prevent their recurrence. [8.1, 8.5.1a, 8.5.2, 8.5.3]

4.1.8. During the Receiving processes, if discrepancies or nonconforming product are discovered or suspected (e.g. wrong goods, wrong quantities, etc.), each discrepancy is noted on the associated packing list, which remains with the goods in a HOLD area while Purchasing personnel are contacted for disposition. (Disposition of discrepant incoming goods and services is addressed in the Purchasing procedure). [8.1, 8.5.1c, 8.7]

4.1.9. If nonconforming product is identified during storage or shipping, it is recorded on Travelers or upon product itself and moved to a HOLD area. It is dispositioned according to the Material Review Board (MRB) routine described in the Production procedure. [8.1, 8.5.1, 8.5.5, 8.7]

4.2. Receiving

4.2.1. Receiving personnel inspect incoming goods for damage while verifying their quantities against their accompanying packing slips. [8.1, 8.5.1c]

4.2.1.1. If damage is apparent, digital photos are taken and immediately submitted to Purchasing personnel. Receiving personnel note damage on carrier's logs. Purchasing personnel evaluate discrepant items and determine disposition, arranging for product return/rework/replacement as appropriate. (See the Supplier Performance section of the Purchasing procedure.) [8.7]

4.2.1.2. Incoming customer property is marked with customer's names or part numbers (if not already labeled) and is received, verified, and stored in the same manner as purchased goods, pending its use. Should customer property be discovered to be discrepant, or if it become damaged or lost, the General Manager will be notified immediately. Management action is initiated, as appropriate, to record details of the issue. (See the Management Action procedure.) Accordingly, the General Manager informs the customer of the problem and actions taken to prevent its recurrence. [8.1, 8.5.1c, 8.5.3, 8.7]

4.2.1.3. Product is verified to be within its shelf life or expiration date, as applicable. [8.1, 8.5.1c]

4.2.1.4. If goods arrive without a packing slip or if Receiving personnel cannot determine the source/destination of the material, management is notified to receive and verify the incoming goods. [8.1, 8.5.1c, 8.7]

4.2.1.5. Product returning from customers will be received and properly identified with a Return Merchandise Authorization number (or at least the customer's name and/or part number) while management is notified for disposition. (See the MRB routine in the Production procedure.) [8.1, 8.5.1h, 8.5.2, 8.5.5, 8.7]

4.2.2. Goods failing the above initial verification are treated as nonconforming product. Accordingly, discrepancies are noted on packing lists, which remain with discrepant product in the receiving HOLD area pending disposition. [8.1, 8.5.1c, 8.7]

4.2.3. Goods passing initial verification are further verified against associated purchasing requirements. Hard-copy records of placed POs are available for materials dedicated to specific jobs with their respective Travelers (as appropriate) in the Receiving files. Packing lists associated with incoming goods are verified to agree with their associated PO requirements, including due-date requirements. (Late shipments are noted on POs; actual date of receipt is noted beside due dates appearing on POs.) Receiving personnel also verify reception of any needed material or process certifications (per Travelers). [8.1, 8.5.1c, 8.5.2, 8.7]

4.2.4. If Travelers indicate QC inspection is required of an incoming item, it is submitted to QC along with its Traveler and packing list. [8.1, 8.5.1b,c]

4.2.5. Incoming QC Inspections

4.2.5.1. QC inspection is required of incoming material, product returning from outsourced processing (including special processing), and/or as specified by Travelers.

Incoming material/parts and associated Traveler packages are submitted to QC personnel. [8.1, 8.5.1a, 8.5.2, (8.4)]

4.2.5.2. QC personnel inspect product according to requirements appearing on Travelers and/or associated blueprints, and in accordance with the C = 0 sampling plan, as appropriate. Inspection results are maintained on inspection reports. Upon successful completion of incoming inspection, associated Travelers are signed and dated by QC personnel to indicate acceptance of product and approval for use. Product is staged for production along with its Traveler packages. QC personnel initial and date packing lists, attach them to their respective POs, and deposit them in the Purchasing inbox. [8.1, 8.5.1a,b,c,d,e, 8.5.2]

4.2.5.3. Product failing QC inspection is treated as nonconforming product. It remains in the QC HOLD area identified by duly-noted packing lists pending disposition by Purchasing personnel. [8.1, 8.5.1c, 8.7]

4.2.6. If no QC inspection is required, and no discrepancies are discovered, Receiving personnel initial and date packing lists to indicate acceptance of the goods and approval for use. Approved packing lists are attached to their respective POs, which are deposited in the Purchasing inbox. The database is updated to reflect "shipment accepted." As applicable, Receiving personnel also initial and date Travelers to indicate acceptance of product and approval for use. [8.1, 8.5.1, 8.5.2]

4.2.7. If an incoming shipment is a partial shipment, its packing list and PO are noted accordingly. Actual quantity received is recorded in the database, on POs, and on packing lists, which are initialed and dated as being received. Packing lists are added to their respective Travelers, as applicable, while associated POs are returned to the Receiving files pending receipt of future shipments. When they arrive, product is inspected, as required, before being stored or joined with its Traveler. (See the Production procedure.) [8.1, 8.5.1, 8.5.2]

4.3. Storage

4.3.1. Incoming product remains in any protective packaging, as appropriate, during storage. Accepted raw materials are stored in raw material storage areas or they are transported to work centers, as appropriate, accompanied by Traveler packages. Accepted tooling is stored in the tool room or delivered directly to work areas, as appropriate. Materials requiring refrigeration (e.g. adhesives) are stored in the tool room refrigerator. [8.1, 8.5.1d, 8.5.4]

4.3.2. Pending use or shipment, product is stored to prevent damage and deterioration according to inventory locations established electronically. Product with shelf life or expiration dates is stored and used according to first-in-first-out methodology. [8.1, 8.5.1s, 8.5.4]

4.3.3. FGI is located in the storage room, which provides protection from production activities; environmental conditions are maintained to preserve product conformity. Product held in FGI is packaged and labeled to display quantity, part number, and revision level. Shelving labels also identify FGI product. [8.1, 8.5.1d, 8.5.4]

4.3.4. All FGI transactions are recorded in the database as they occur. FGI is assessed routinely during cycle counts. Any damage or deterioration of product discovered during storage will result in the initiation of management action. Affected product will be treated as nonconforming product, to be dispositioned according to the Production procedure. [8.1, 8.5.1, 8.7]

4.3.5. Product is released to customers from FGI via Stock Shippers, which are provided by Sales personnel. Each Stock Shipper shares the same job number and product identification information as the Traveler associated with product build.

Stock Shippers serve as Travelers during shipping. [8.1, 8.5.1a (8.6)]

4.4. Shipping

4.4.1. Product Destined for Outsourced processing

4.4.1.1. When product is due for outsourced processing, the parts and accompanying Traveler packages are submitted to Shipping personnel. Using the database, Shipping personnel access electronic copies of approved POs. (See the Purchasing procedure.) [8.1, 8.5.1a (8.4)]

4.4.1.2. POs corresponding to Travelers' job numbers and operation numbers are printed, as is a copy of any documentation that may be required by suppliers (e.g. drawings or specifications), as specified on Travelers. (These are available in electronic part number folders, as applicable.) [8.1, 8.5.1a, 8.5.2]

4.4.1.3. Shipping personnel verify that part quantities agree with Traveler data and electronic inventory data while packaging. The Production Manager is notified to resolve any count discrepancies. [8.1, 8.5.1a,c, 8.5.2, 8.7]

4.4.1.4. Parts are packaged to prevent damage during transport, and then released to outsourced processing along with their respective POs (and drawings/specifications, as applicable). If Travelers indicate that special packaging requirements apply, product is packaged accordingly. Upon completion of packaging, shipping personnel initial and date the appropriate spaces on Travelers to indicate part counts are correct and packaging is complete, and that any required documents are included. [8.1, 8.5.1a, 8.5.2, 8.5.4]

4.4.1.5. Product is either delivered to outsourced processing via a company vehicle, picked up by processors, or is shipped to suppliers via commercial carriers according to arrangements appearing on Travelers. [8.1, 8.5.1]

4.4.1.6. Product returning from outsourced processing is received and verified according to the Receiving procedure (described previously). [8.1, 8.5.1 (8.4)]

4.4.2. Finished Product

4.4.2.1. Finished product is submitted to the Shipping area accompanied by Traveler packages. (See the Production procedure.) Finished product is identified by final QC approval appearing on Travelers. Travelers also indicate finished quantities, identifying quantities destined for shipping and those destined for FGI. (Production personnel enter the same information electronically. See the Production procedure.) [8.1, 8.5.1a, 8.5.2, (8.6)]

4.4.2.2. If Travelers identify special packaging or labeling requirements, product is packaged or labeled accordingly. Absent such requirements, product is packaged to preserve product conformity during storage and transport using suitable materials available in the Shipping area. Quantities are verified to agree with Traveler data and electronic inventory data as product is being packaged. Any discrepancies are brought to the attention of the Production Manager or General Manger for resolution before proceeding. [8.1, 8.5.1a,d, 8.5.2, 8.5.4, 8.7]

4.4.2.3. Using the database, Shipping personnel generate packing lists in duplicate to accompany outgoing packages and shipping labels. Shipping labels are attached to outgoing packages. Shipments involving more than one package are labeled with box number and total packages (e.g. 1 of 3, 2 of 3, and 3 of 3). Product destined for FGI is packaged, labeled, and placed into FGI (as described previously). [8.1, 8.5.1a, 8.5.2, 8.5.4]

4.4.2.4. Finished product is either delivered to customers using a company vehicle, picked up by customers, or shipped to customers via commercial carriers according to arrangements appearing on Travelers and packing lists.

(When packing lists are generated, FGI data is automatically updated to relieve quantities from inventory.) [8.1, 8.5.1]

4.4.2.5. Upon delivery or pick-up, a customer representative signs two copies of packing lists to indicate delivery acceptance. Customers retain one copy while Shipping personnel retain the other. [8.1, 8.5.1a]

4.4.2.6. Packing lists are placed in the Sales inbox. When product is shipped, customers' copies of packing lists are affixed to boxes using envelope stickers; company copies are initialed and dated by Receiving personnel and placed in the Sales inbox along with carrier's records of transfer. [8.1, 8.5.1]

4.4.2.7. Once product has been released, Shipping personnel initial and date Travelers to indicate product release. Travelers are then considered closed. The database is updated to reflect released shipments. Closed Travelers are deposited into the Closed Travelers file in the Production Control office. [8.1, 8.5.1]

4.5. Change History

4.5.1. Original issue: 09/15/13

Production

According to the conformity matrix, the following nine realization requirements of ISO 9001:2015 pertain to the Production process and are to be addressed and met by the Production procedure:

8.1, Operational planning and control,

8.5.1, Control of production and service provision,

8.5.2, Identification and traceability,

8.5.3, Property belonging to customers or external providers,

8.5.4, Preservation,

8.5.5, Post-delivery activities,

8.5.6, Control of changes,

8.6, Release of product and services, and

8.7, Nonconforming outputs.

One of the Production Supervisors and the Production Manager explained the process. Here's what we came up with:

PRODUCTION   Rev J

1. Objectives and Purpose

1.1 Objective

1.1.1. Process objective: Aligning with the system objectives of customer satisfaction, quality product release, and on time delivery, the primary objective of the Production process is to produce conforming product in a timely manner, while preserving product conformity throughout processing.

1.1.2. Performance objectives: A primary objective of the production process is to consistently output product meeting applicable requirements as effectively and efficiently as possible. More specific performance objectives are established, measured, and tracked as prescribed during Management Review. (See the QMS Management procedure.)

1.2. The purpose of this procedure is to describe the controlled conditions under which Production activities are planned and conducted to ensure that customer requirements are met, including verification activities. This procedure also addresses subcontracted processing and maintenance activities, as well as the treatment of nonconforming product discovered during processing.

2. Responsibility and Applicability

2.1. This procedure applies to the Production Manager, Production Supervisors, and the rest of Production personnel, who are responsible for, and authorized to, perform their assigned activities and verifications, including storage, handling, and preservation of product. All Production personnel are also responsible for, and authorized to stop processing when problems are discovered and to control further processing while management is notified for resolution.

2.2. The Production Manager is responsible for, and authorized to perform, direct, and oversee activities related to production. The President, the Production Manager, and the QC Manager are responsible for, and authorized to disposition nonconforming product. (In cases when product is obviously scrap, Production personnel are authorized to disposition it as such.)

2.3. The President is responsible for ensuring that this procedure is accurate, understood and implemented effectively. This procedure may not be changed without the authorization of the President.

3. Inputs and Outputs

3.1. Inputs to the production process include product accepted through the Receiving process and production priorities established via Manufacturing Requirements Planning (MRP) data and the job list. Inputs also include Travelers generated during the Sales process.

3.2. Outputs include finished product meeting customer requirements and the associated records. Evidence of product verification and release appear on completed Travelers and in the MRP system. Inspection records (e.g. First Article Sheets, CMM reports) provide further evidence of product conformity, as applicable. Occasionally, nonconforming product is an output of the production process, as are the records of its identification and disposition.

4. Procedure

4.1. General

4.1.1. Production personnel perform departmental activities according to documented work instructions (e.g. posted work aids, flow charts, Travelers, etc.) and according to instructions to which they have been trained. (See the Training procedure.)

4.1.2. Production personnel identify the need to purchase resources needed for the operation of the Shipping and Receiving process, including tooling and consumables. These are brought to the attention of Production Supervisors or the Production Manager. As appropriate, needed items are recorded on the "Tools to Order" list. Once the identified items are confirmed to be needed, they are procured according to the Purchasing procedure. [7.5.1]

4.1.3. Documents used during processing are controlled according to the Document and Record Control procedure (and this procedure), as are records generated during processing.

4.1.4. Employees handle and store items carefully to ensure their own safety and the safety of others. All employees involved in product handling and storage do so to preserve product conformity and to maintain product identification. Appropriate handling methods and transport equipment are used at all times.

4.1.5. Personnel who are required to use calibrated devices are trained in their selection, handling, and use to ensure continued accuracy of measurements and continued fitness of the instruments. Such devices are controlled according to the Calibration procedure.

4.1.6. Product is identified by the following features, as appropriate: part numbers, job numbers, labeling/markings on product, containers, or storage locations, physical appearance, associated Travelers and drawings, and its location in-process.

4.1.7. Customer property is handled, used, stored and preserved in the same manner as purchased product. If any customer property is lost or damaged, it will be brought to the attention of the Production Manager or Preproduction personnel, who will initiate Management Action and inform the customer of the problem as well as any actions taken to prevent its recurrence. When customers supply material, accompanying Travelers identify it as customer-supplied.

4.1.8. Travelers and blueprints identify processing requirements for any given order, including outsourced processing requirements, as well as any special customer requirements, such as those for traceability, product identification/handling, packaging or shipping, etc. Outputs of each processing step are verified before release to subsequent steps. Operators initial Travelers to indicate completed and verified operations, including the quantity of conforming and nonconforming parts. This information is also entered to the MRP system.

4.1.9. When product is suspected of being nonconforming, personnel discovering the problem note the quantity of affected parts on Travelers. Suspected nonconforming product is segregated from conforming product at the workstation, where it remains while management is contacted for disposition. Nonconforming product will not be used, further processed, or distributed without the approval of management. Nonconforming product is dispositioned according to section 4.5 of this procedure.

4.1.10. When nonconforming product is obviously scrap, Production personnel are authorized to scrap it. Scrap quantities are recorded on Travelers and in the MRP system.

4.1.11. Scrapped parts are disposed of (or recycled) upon operation completion, if not immediately. (Marked with red permanent marker pending disposal, as appropriate.) If scrapped parts can be used as set-up parts, they are marked "S/U" (in red). Set-up parts remain with the balance of the order until they are no longer needed, at which point they are scrapped. Should such parts be retained for future use, it will be marked also with job number or part number and revision number.

4.2. Production Planning

4.2.1. The Production Manager reviews Travelers held in the "pending approval" queue for adequacy, accuracy, effectiveness, and efficiency before releasing them for use in Production. (See the Sales procedure.) Only Travelers electronically bearing the approval of the Production Manager are further released within the MRP system.

4.2.2. The Quality Manager reviews Travelers in the "pending approval" queue that contain "notes" to assure compliance with any special requirements pertaining to the order. Any special customer requirements for inspections, sampling, critical dimensions, etc., as well as notes concerning handling, preservation, any needed training, etc. appear within the "notes" section (see the Sales procedure). Once notes are verified to be clear, and the ability to meet all special requirements has been appropriately planned and confirmed, the Quality Manager electronically approves Travelers. Travelers containing notes must bear the approval of the Quality Manager before being released for use in Production.

4.2.3. After material has been ordered via the Purchasing process, Travelers and job lists developed during the Sales process are placed into the appropriate in/out boxes, along with their respective blueprints and any other relevant documentation. Materials dedicated to each order are received, cut (as necessary), and verified according to the Shipping and

Receiving procedure. Accordingly, materials are logged into the MRP system and made available for processing.

4.2.4. Travelers requiring CNC programming (e.g. new or modified orders) are submitted to programming personnel, who develop necessary CNC programs. Completed, verified programs are saved to reflect part number, revision, and operation number, and programmer initials indicating approval and date of approval. (Once saved, any revisions to CNC programs overwrite previous data, while approval dates reflect most recent revision.)

4.2.5. Based upon order due dates appearing in the MRP system and weekly job lists provided by Sales personnel, the Production Manager determines production priorities.

4.2.6. When changes to open orders are accepted (see the Sales procedure), the Production Manager directly notifies affected Production personnel of specific changes. As appropriate, the Production Manager or Supervisors reviews updated processing requirements with affected personnel to ensure requirements are clearly understood and will be applied. (Initials of management providing and personnel receiving such training is written upon Travelers as evidence of such reviews when they are required.)

4.3. Production

4.3.1. Using the MRP system and barcodes appearing on Travelers, Production personnel wand into assigned operations. Needed materials are transported to the appropriate workstations. Production personnel acquire any needed tooling according to CNC program call-outs. If material traceability is required (according to Travelers), Production personnel ensure material is positively identified as the traceable material (via job numbers and/or purchase order numbers).

4.3.2. Production personnel process orders using suitable equipment available in production areas, and as specified by

Travelers and set-up sheets. Personnel wand into the set-up operation and proceed to set-up equipment for the run according to set-up sheets, as applicable.

4.3.3. Once set-up is complete and verified, First Article (FA) parts are produced to further verify proper set-up and product conformity. FA parts are submitted to Quality Control (QC).

4.3.4. FA Inspection

4.3.4.1. Upon receiving an FA part and Traveler, QC personnel use the $C = 0$ sampling plan to determine sampling requirements for that production run. QC personnel record sampling requirements upon on their respective Travelers.

4.3.4.2. QC personnel proceed to inspect FA parts according to requirements appearing on or referenced by blueprints and associated Travelers, while results are recorded on FA sheets or CMM reports, as appropriate.

4.3.4.3. QC personnel indicate acceptable results in the MRP system and upon Travelers, which are returned to Production personnel.

4.3.4.4. QC personnel notify Operators of any detected problems. Operators adjust equipment as necessary and produce new FA parts. If modified programming is required, or the problem cannot be resolved, management is notified for resolution.

4.3.5. Once QC has approved FA parts, Production personnel wand into the operation and run production parts according to requirements appearing on blueprints in quantities specified by Travelers. Should tool changes or other significant process changes or unplanned events occur, affected parts are submitted to QC and treated as FA parts (and noted as such on Travelers).

4.3.6. Critical dimensions

4.3.6.1. If blueprints identify critical dimensions via highlighting and "Critical Dimensions" stamps, operators are required to 100% inspect these dimensions unless otherwise specified. In such cases, Production personnel are required to check-out and use approved QC devices, and they are authorized to record actual measurements on blueprints in the spaces created by Critical Dimensions stamps (and in such a way as to not obscure data on the prints).

4.3.6.2. Measurements are signed and dated by those responsible; the backside of blueprints may be used to record measurements, as necessary. Operators also observe any other special inspection instructions appearing on blueprints or Travelers, as applicable. (Such instructions bear the approval of the QC Manager.)

4.3.7. Upon completion of each operation, Production personnel verify that resulting product meets applicable requirements, including dimensions and tolerances appearing on blueprints. After inspecting parts, Production personnel initial/date Travelers and wand out of the operation. The number of conforming and nonconforming parts is recorded both on Travelers and in the MRP system. Accompanied by their Travelers, parts are submitted to QC.

4.3.8. As before, QC personnel inspect product according to blueprint requirements. QC personnel indicate acceptable results upon Travelers (and in the MRP system), which are returned to Production for further processing. Actual measurements are recorded using CMM reports or FA sheets. Any nonconforming product discovered during QC inspections is dispositioned per 4.5.

4.3.9. When outsourced processing is necessary according to Travelers, product to be processed and its paperwork are submitted to Shipping personnel for packaging and shipment to approved suppliers per the Shipping and Receiving procedure. Product returning from outsourced processing is verified also per the Shipping and Receiving procedure. Only product verified to meet requirements is released to subsequent processing (as evidenced by QC approval on Travelers and MRP data).

4.3.10. Upon completion of the last production operation required of Travelers, product is submitted to QC for final inspection. QC inspection finished product as described previously. Product failing inspection is treated as nonconforming product, while product passing inspection is authorized for release to customers. (Records are retained on Travelers and in MRP.) Finished product submitted to Shipping personnel for processing according to the Shipping and Receiving procedure.

4.4. Maintenance

4.4.1. When production machinery/equipment breaks down or fails, it will be repaired or replaced at the discretion of management. Any repairs or new equipment will be ordered and fulfilled according to the Purchasing procedure.

4.4.2. Preventive maintenance is performed on company vehicles that are used to deliver product to customers. Vehicle maintenance is performed routinely by commercial suppliers, the records of which are retained in the vehicle maintenance files.

4.4.3. Preventive maintenance routinely by suppliers (according to suppliers' scheduling) is retained by office personnel according to the Record Retention Form.

4.5. Nonconforming Product

4.5.1. Nonconforming product is brought to the attention of the President, Production Manager, or QC Manager, who evaluates it and determines its disposition. Possible dispositions include:

scrap, rework, use with approved concession, return to supplier, or use as is without further action.

- **Scrap** means that the product will be disposed of and replacement parts will be made, as appropriate, after any necessary adjustments are made to prevent recurrence of the nonconforming condition. In such cases, a new Traveler is used to produce the replacement order.

- **Rework** means that though the product does not meet the applicable requirements, it can be reworked to meet those requirements. In such cases, rework instructions (from the Production Manager) are recorded on Rework Travelers, which are returned to the appropriate Production personnel. The product is reworked accordingly and verified against the criteria by which it originally failed before further processing. Records of re-verification appear on Rework Travelers and associated MRP records.

- **Use as is under concession** means that the product does not meet all applicable requirements. In such cases, an email documenting nonconformities are submitted to customers, as required. Alternatively or additionally, customer-supplied deviation/waiver documentation may be used.

- **Return to supplier** means that the product will be reworked or replaced by the supplier; Purchasing personnel arrange for the return of the material.

- **Use as is without further action** means that the product has been determined to meet applicable requirements and is not nonconforming product.

4.5.2. Disposition is recorded on Travelers and in the MRP system, while associated product is processed accordingly. Records of Travelers are maintained in the Traveler file. Management initiates Management Action, as appropriate.

4.5.3. Product returning from customers due to deficiencies discovered after delivery or use will have been arranged according to the RMA routine described in the Sales procedure. Returned product is evaluated and dispositioned as described above. Should product that has already been shipped to the customer be suspected of being nonconforming, the issue will be brought to the attention of management, who will contact the customer immediately to resolve the issue.

4.6. Change History

4.6.1. Original issue: 09/15/13

While no procedure is perfect, the above procedures describe Bob's realization processes at an appropriate level to assure consistency in process performance, and conformity to the applicable requirements can be plainly seen. Properly written QMS procedures can take many forms; for example, a flow diagram could cover this process. This format was chosen to provide an illustration of how current processing meets applicable requirements.

In Bob's case, since the "Production" and "Shipping and Receiving" procedures were written in process fashion, these two procedures replaced nine standard-based procedures, relieving the organization of seven QMS documents. Not only is the resulting system more sensible, it's much leaner. When processes are properly defined they can be systemically improved upon, which is important from a quality perspective.

Quality Manual

A properly defined QMS is a system of processes that can use the PDCA cycle to sensibly improve the processes and the QMS as a whole. Other quality tools such as Six Sigma and Lean can be applied across the system as part of the routine operation and improvement of QMS processes and activities. Until the process approach is adopted, procedures based upon a standard's requirements will continue failing to properly define processes, fouling proper application of the PDCA cycle to the QMS and its processes.

An organization already certified to ISO 9001 using a twenty-element approach or the "mandatory six" approach would be wise to recognize that its QMS documentation does not accurately reflect its own organizational structures. Such documentation is often counterproductive and not conducive to good quality management. Perhaps a classic case of "groupthink," it is now up to quality professionals and organizational management to overcome this common obstacle and work together in defining sensible QMSs.

Regarding the sensible definition of a QMS, again remember Bob. Like most organizations, Bob's quality manual—the document defining Bob's QMS—is based upon the clauses of the standard. To Bob, the following advice might be appropriate:

"About your quality manual: Notice that it's structured according to the standard. While this is a widely accepted practice by ISO professionals, does it reflect a process approach? Does it accurately describe your system of processes? It is clearly an index for an auditor to find conformity, rather than a description of a system of processes affecting quality. Rather than describing the system and processes and their management toward improvement, the purpose of your manual seems to involve methodically providing an answer to each requirement.

What would you base your manual upon if there were no ISO 9001? Why not base it upon your system and processes as they currently operate?

When the standard was originally released by ISO, the authors of the standard didn't intend for ISO 9001 to be prescriptive regarding QMS documentation—beyond requiring that you establish some kind of documentation. The structure laid out by guidance documents at the time suggested three levels of documentation: level one, quality manual (a policy-type document), level two procedures (implementing the policies within processes affecting quality), and level three procedures (work instructions, forms, or work aids, etc., specifying how particular activities are properly performed). I suggest we follow this guidance when we write your manual.

ISO 9000:2015 addresses the process approach and a systemic approach to management. It suggests that activities are best viewed and managed as processes, while processes are best viewed and managed as being part of a system. As it sits, your system is composed of five realization processes: Sales, Purchasing, Receiving, Production, and Shipping. Because the Shipping process and the Receiving process are contained in one document called the Shipping and Receiving procedure, we have only four procedures dedicated to realization processes.

We already have six procedures dedicated to support processes: Document and Record Control, Internal Audits, Management Action, Calibration, Training, and Management Review. You can keep these, as you're used to them. Notice that the Document and Record Control and the Management Action procedures each address two processes, much like the Shipping and Receiving procedure.

For now, all told, we have 13 processes, as we have defined them, using ten procedures. Let's write the manual to describe the QMS, how it's managed, and who is responsible for what. Then, we can relate it to the processes as we have documented them. We will treat conformity to ISO 9001 requirements as a secondary concern. In the manual, requirements can be addressed at the top level, knowing that appropriate detail can be included within procedures (according to our handy conformity matrix).

As far as ISO 9001 requirements are concerned, we could get away with a one-page quality manual if we wanted to. But let's write something that makes sense to you, something that shows you care enough to define a few things, and something you could show to a customer wondering about the robustness of your QMS. But remember: we are writing a quality manual, not a conformity manual.

Having said that, let's write the manual to describe the system and its processes first, and then pull out the standard to ensure requirements are being met. At that time, we can adjust language as necessary and prudent to more clearly demonstrate conformity."

Sample Quality Manual

Bob wanted something fairly formal and presentable to customers— not too long and not too short—something understandable to management and personnel, and yet clearly compliant with ISO 9001 requirements. Worried that his customers or auditors would not easily understand how documentation based upon processes meets all requirements of the standard, he wanted enough "ISOese" in a quality manual so they could easily connect the dots. And he wanted to basically keep the existing support structure. With that, we went to work on the Quality Manual. Here's what we came up with:

Table of Contents

1. Company Information

Bob's Machine Shop was founded in 1980, specializing in contract manufacturing and engineering. For more than twenty-five years, Bob's Machine Shop has produced high quality precision CNC-machined components, parts, and assemblies for a wide variety of industries.

Currently Bob's Machine Shop operates in a 12,000 square-foot facility; a variety of CNC machining centers. The existing organizational knowledge, infrastructure and work environment have been confirmed to be adequate by a history of successful operations, evidenced by years of previously processed quality work. Future additions to the infrastructure or work environment will be qualified according to the Management Review and Purchasing procedures.

2. Quality Management System

2.1. Success Factors

As a contract manufacturer, the issues most relevant to our success involve our ability to consistently satisfy customers with quality products delivered on time.

In order to profit from consistently provide customers with timely, quality products, issues posing risk to meeting our quality objectives include: our ability to meet customer requirements (including applicable statutory/regulatory requirements), the availability of resources to accommodate demand, and the effectiveness and efficiency of operations.

Information about these internal and external issues is routinely reviewed, monitored and acted upon by personnel and management working in primary processes: Sales, Purchasing, Shipping and Receiving, and Production.

Sales personnel review customer orders to determine customer requirements (including any related statutory or regulatory requirements relevant to product or processing), assuring company capability, while monitoring the sales forecast and production schedule to assure the company also has the capacity to meet customer requirements before order acceptance (see the Sales procedure).

Purchasing personnel source and procure any needed materials, tooling, or equipment to be available when needed by Production (see the Purchasing procedure), monitoring stock levels, inventory levels, production demand and the sales forecast as appropriate.

Production management assure production processes (including Production as well as Shipping and Receiving) are operating effectively and efficiently according to performance information as it becomes available (monitoring set-up times, turn times, throughput, and defect rates). (See the Shipping and Receiving procedure and the Production procedure.)

All process owners assure competent human resources are available to conduct processing competently according to established procedures (see the Training procedure).

A QMS and performance objectives have been established by top management to promote stable process performance and to provide a foundation for process improvement as deemed necessary. Appropriate actions are taken to assure timely delivery of product to customers, to address risks and opportunities, to improve performance, all in an effort to enhance customer satisfaction.

2.2. Scope

The QMS applies to operations conducted on the premises of Bob's Machine Shop. The boundary of the QMS is understood as being defined by the processes comprising the system (see section 5 and [Figure 17]). The scope of the QMS, considering the above success factors and our scope of operations, is defined as follows:

Sales and manufacturing of precision-machined products to customer specifications

Since Bob's Machine Shop does not design products that are sold to customers, design is outside the boundary of the QMS; a design process is not included within the scope of the QMS. Therefore, the design requirements of ISO 9001:2015 (8.3) are not applicable.

Also, since no process operated by Bob's Machine Shop produces unverifiable outputs, the requirements of ISO 9001:2015 (8.5.1 f) are not applicable within our scope of operations. However, the Purchasing procedure describes controls exerted over suppliers providing special processes, while the Receiving procedure describes verifications required of product arriving from special processing.

The remainder of ISO 9001:2015 requirements are applicable; these requirements are applied during internal audits to assure QMS conformity.

3. Leadership

3.1. Commitment to quality

Top management is committed to maintaining and improving the QMS in order to continually satisfy customers by providing them with product that meets their requirements. Top management is accountable to all interested parties for the performance of the company and the effectiveness of the QMS.

Top Management (the Owner and General Manager) ensures that customer requirements are met with the intension of enhancing customer satisfaction. This commitment is demonstrated by the development and implementation of the QMS, by formulating the Quality Policy, and by establishing measurable objectives against which QMS performance is evaluated and acted upon in an effort to improve processing and the resulting products. Top management ensures that employees understand the importance of meeting requirements, particularly those of our customers.

Top management also demonstrates a commitment to quality by conducting periodic Management Reviews of the QMS and its processes. Based on factual information regarding performance and other feedback from customers, and in consideration of future customer needs, management allocates resources as necessary to ensure conformity of product, to improve the QMS, its processes, and resulting product, in order to promote customer satisfaction.

Finally, top management demonstrates leadership and commitment to quality by systemically applying plan-do-check-act to the system and its processes. The QMS applies a process approach to quality management, integrating QMS requirements into our business processes, whether primary or support.

Risk-based thinking is applied as part of the process approach to assure operations are not only effective, but effectively and efficiently *managed*. Accordingly, our system is viewed and documented as a system of processes satisfying customers (effectively managing risks that would result in unsatisfactory performance).

3.2. Knowledge and Communication

Knowledge and communication are essential to successful operations.

Knowledge. Internal knowledge relevant to operations is captured in or referenced by QMS documentation, including this manual, associated procedures, work instructions, training requirements, and other process documentation. The QA Library contains all relevant standards and customer specifications; periodicals containing current industry news and best practices are always available in the QA Library.

As improvements are planned to remain competitive and profitable (see the QMS Management procedure), and as technological advances are realized, updates to existing organizational knowledge are reflected in updated training requirements and process documentation.

Personnel are provided new or updated training as appropriate (see the Training procedure). Accordingly, arrangements are made to provide personnel with education from external sources as necessary.

Communication. Appropriate channels have been established to accommodate QMS communications. QMS procedures describe in detail the responsibilities for internal and external communications, including who communicates what, when, and to whom; methods of communication are also established.

To provide an overview: Sales personnel communicate with customers regarding product requirements; as customer orders are accepted, order information is communicated to Purchasing personnel and Production management personnel.

Purchasing personnel communicate relevant resource requirements to suppliers, while Production management assembles information to be communicated to Production personnel within Traveler folders (including Travelers, blueprints, and any other necessary process documentation).

Receiving personnel inspect incoming materials according to product/service requirements communicated by Purchasing; accepted product is made available to Production.

Production personnel set-up and run customer orders according to information contained in Traveler folders; during production and upon completion, performance information is recorded on Travelers; quality assurance personnel collect relevant data from Travelers, which is communicated to Production management during production meetings, and ultimately to top management during QMS Management meetings.

All QMS process owners communicate process performance information to top management during QMS Management meetings, as does the Quality Manager. Also during QMS Management meetings, performance information arising from external sources (including customer satisfaction data) is gathered by Sales personnel and communicated to top management.

Performance information and objectives for improvement are recorded in QMS Management meeting minutes; appropriate information is summarized and posted on the Quality Bulletin Board and reviewed with personnel as appropriate.

When improvement initiatives result in process modifications, changes are communicated, as appropriate, via updated QMS procedures, new/updated training requirements, and updated process documentation (e.g., Travelers, blueprints, Inspection Reports, etc.), as well as Quality Bulletin Board postings.

3.3. Quality Policy

Top management's commitment to meeting requirements, satisfying customers, and improving the QMS, its processes and resulting products is reflected in the following quality policy:

Bob's Machine Shop strives to satisfy customers by supplying them with quality products that are delivered on time. We continually strive to improve our products and processes in order to remain a good supplier to our customers.

Top management reviews the above policy periodically during Management Review to ensure its continuing suitability, ensuring that it remains appropriate for the company, that it includes a commitment to comply with requirements and to continually improve the QMS, and that it provides a foundation for measurable objectives against which performance can be evaluated.

Top management also ensures that all employees understand the policy, how it applies in their work, and how their performance relates to the achievement of quality policy objectives. The policy is posted on the Quality Bulletin Board.

3.4. Quality Objectives

Top management has established measurable objectives for QMS performance that are derived from the policy, taking into account applicable requirements. Such objectives serve as a foundation for reviewing performance at both the process and system level, in order to apply the Plan-Do-Check-Act cycle to both the QMS processes and to the system of processes in aggregate. System objectives include customer satisfaction, on-time delivery, and quality. Top management encourages all personnel to contribute to achieving these objectives.

Key objectives and measurements are addressed during Management Review meetings, along with an indication of a timeframe for their achievement, and are used to implement the quality policy. Key objectives and measurements are posted on the Quality Bulletin Board.

4. QMS Overview

Bob's QMS, like the documentation describing it, is structured around the processes affecting the quality of products offered by Bob's Machine Shop. The QMS has been developed and implemented to promote quality and improvement, and is managed to meet the requirements of ISO 9001:2008. See [Figure 15].

The QMS can be viewed as a system of processes that fall into two general categories: primary processes and support processes. The primary processes involve product realization activities directly affecting quality of product intended for customers these include (in general sequence): Sales, Purchasing, Receiving, Production, and Shipping. Support processes are those necessary for the successful operation and control of the primary processes and the QMS as a whole. These operate in parallel with primary process, and thus are not sequential: Calibration, Management Action, Document and Record Control, Internal Audits, Training, and QMS Management. Overviews of these QMS processes appear in Section 5 of this manual.

The need for outsourced processing is identified during the Sales and/or during production planning. (See the Sales and Production procedures.) Outsourced processing is procured according to the Purchasing procedure. Product destined for outsourced processing is staged in the Shipping and Receiving area per the Production procedure. It is packaged and released to suppliers according to the Shipping and Receiving procedure, which also describes requirements for verifying incoming product arriving from outsourced processing before its acceptance.

A documented procedure has been established, implemented and maintained for each QMS process, regardless of whether it is a primary or a support process. Each procedure identifies the inputs to and outputs of the process, and describes how those inputs are transformed into their respective outputs under controlled conditions. Each procedure also identifies responsibilities and authorities of personnel performing the process, as well as those responsible for measuring or monitoring process performance against established objectives, and for reacting appropriately to ensure the quality of the product and to promote improvement.

The Plan-Do-Check-Act cycle applies to each QMS process, whether primary or support, as well as to the system of processes in aggregate.

4.1. Responsibilities and Authorities

Top management ensures that responsibilities and authorities are defined and communicated to all employees. Top management is ultimately responsible for the quality of Bob's products and processes. Top management is responsible for ensuring confidentiality of customer-contracted products and projects under development, and related product information.

A general description of responsibilities and authorities associated with each company position follows. Such responsibilities and authorities are further described elsewhere in this manual and in specific operating procedures. Top management supports all levels of management to be effective and successful in their areas of responsibility.

- The Owner and General Manager perform and oversee Sales, Purchasing, Production, and Shipping and Receiving activities.

As top management, the Owner also conducts QMS Management meetings.

- The Sales Manager performs the Sales process, including customer service.

- The Purchasing Manager performs and oversees the Purchasing process and purchasing personnel.

- The Quality Manager performs and oversees Calibration and inspection activities associated with Production, Shipping, and Receiving. The Quality Manager also performs Document and Record Control, Internal Audits, Management Action, and Training activities.

- The Quality Manager is responsible for and authorized to ensure the QMS conforms to current ISO 9001 requirements and that processes are performing as expected. The Quality Manager is also responsible for reporting performance information and improvement opportunities to top management during QMS Management meetings, and for promoting customer focus throughout the company.

- The Production Manager oversees the Production process and the Shipping and Receiving processes, shared responsibilities with the General Manager. The Production Manager also oversees the Production Supervisors and the Shipping and Receiving Supervisors.

- Production, Shipping, and Receiving personnel are responsible for performing operations according to established procedures and per the direction of management (including Supervisors).

Top management is responsible for ensuring that personnel who employ statistical techniques throughout the organization understand basic statistical concepts. (Competence with statistical concepts is reflected in training records, as appropriate.)

Though responsibilities and authorities ultimately reside with top management, they are delegated to competent personnel as necessary. All personnel who perform, manage, and/or verify work are responsible for the quality of products produced by Bob's Machine Shop. All employees are responsible for complying with documented procedures and the direction of management. All employees are authorized to identify and record problems relating to products, processes, and the quality system as a whole, and to provide suggestions for improvement or recommendations for solving problems by initiating actions according to the Management Action procedure. All employees are also responsible for cooperating fully with Internal Audits.

Production personnel are responsible for ensuring control over their activities and to complete work in a responsible and safe manner. All employees are responsible for maintaining the premises in a state of order, cleanliness, and repair consistent with product and processing needs. They are also responsible for identifying nonconforming product, stopping production as necessary, and controlling further processing until management has been promptly notified and the problem has been corrected.

4.2. Quality Planning

Top management ensures that QMS planning occurs according to planned arrangements, taking into consideration our success factors (2.1), risks and opportunities, and ensuring that QMS planning is carried out in order to meet the requirements of our customers as well as our own internal requirements and objectives.

QMS planning occurs at two levels to assure intended results are achieved: the process level and the system level. At both levels, risks and opportunities are acted upon to assure intended results are achieved, making desirable results more likely while reducing likelihood of errors or other undesirable effects or results, in an effort to achieve improvement.

While actions to address the above risks and opportunities are routinely taken by personnel as part of their everyday operations, actions affecting how we operate (defined by the Quality Manual and QMS procedures) are Management Actions; these are taken according to the Management Action procedure, which ensures these actions employ risk-based thinking and that they are integrated into QMS processing (and process documentation, as appropriate). The Management Action procedure assures the effectiveness of actions taken.

Planning at the process level focuses on processing a particular order to ensure conformity of the product to applicable requirements according to customer specifications and acceptance criteria. This planning is to establish processes and documentation specific to the product, and to identify product-specific resource requirements. This level of planning results in quality plans (e.g. Travelers), which identify particular processing steps, required verifications to ensure conformity of the product, records demonstrating conformity, methods for reacting when planned arrangements are not achieved, and any contingency planning requirements or post-delivery activities. (Post-delivery activities currently include honoring warranty agreements, based upon workmanship standards, product liability, and product life expectancy.)

As required by customers, Travelers reflect supplemental instructions to comply with customer requirements for processing control (e.g. sampling, in-process inspection requirements, statistical process control, handling, labeling, any post-delivery activities, etc.). In cases when customers require sampling or statistical process control (SPC), customers must provide or specify document and record formats, and must provide training regarding the performance of SPC and the reporting of results. (Reception of such training will be reflected in Training Records.)

As a contract manufacturer, Bob's Machine Shop does not design product. Should requirements for design arise, appropriately qualified design contractors will fulfill these requirements.

Planning at the system level involves establishing the QMS processes and infrastructure necessary to meet general requirements of customers, focusing on the ability of the system to effectively and efficiently meet such requirements. This planning is conducted with a multidisciplinary approach, and takes into consideration facility and equipment plans, plant layout to optimize material flow, handling, and value added use of floor space. Such planning results in system-level processes and procedures that represent the planned arrangements described by QMS documentation.

The above system level planning has already been implemented and the resulting arrangements are currently adequate to meet the requirements of our customers. In general, the quality plan for processing routine orders is to process them in a manner consistent with the existing planned arrangements described by QMS procedures. Where requested orders, products or projects containing significantly new or modified requirements are to be pursued, top management will ensure that quality planning is conducted, and that such planning is implemented and appropriately documented before promising to supply new or significantly modified products. (See the QMS Management procedure.)

Where changes to the QMS are planned, due to changes in technology or in the market, changes caused by suppliers, changes to processes, procedures, or product requirements, introduction of new processes or products, etc., top management will ensure that the integrity of the QMS is maintained to ensure conformity of product to requirements. The full impact of proposed changes will be determined, as appropriate, including resource requirements and changes to existing organizational responsibilities and authorities.

Planned changes will be verified and validated to ensure conformity to customer requirements before implementation. Such QMS planning and change management is conducted during Management Review, or more frequently as circumstances dictate according to the Management Action procedure. (See the QMS Management and Management Actions procedures.)

Currently no special processes are in use, meaning that no existing process produces results that cannot be fully verified by subsequent monitoring or measurement, or where product deficiencies become apparent only after use. If such processes are to be employed, top management will ensure that criteria for review and approval of the process and equipment are established and that such processes are validated to demonstrate their ability to achieve planned results. Top management will ensure that specific methods are developed and documented, records are developed, competence is addressed, and such processes are revalidated as necessary to ensure their continuing suitability.

Though uncommon, customer requirements calling for special processing are fulfilled using outsourced special processes. Control of outsourced special processing is addressed in the Purchasing procedure, which describes how requirements for special processing are specified to qualified suppliers, and in the Receiving procedure, which describes how product returning from special processing is verified to meet specified requirements.

4.3. Resource Management

Top management ensures that resource requirements are determined and met where they are needed to effectively establish, implement, operate and control QMS processes, to maintain and improve the QMS, and to achieve customer satisfaction by meeting their requirements.

QMS resource requirements include human resources (including personnel and training resources), infrastructure resources (including buildings, workspace, process and safety equipment, operating supplies, measuring devices, documentation, and supporting services and utilities), and work environment resources (including safety, ergonomic and human/physical aspects of work being performed).

In consideration of existing resource capabilities and constraints, resource needs may be identified within any QMS process, or they may arise in connection with QMS Management meetings, management actions, internal audits, employee observations, etc. Such needs are fulfilled according to the Purchasing procedure.

4.4. Monitoring, Measurement, and Analysis

Monitoring and measurement methods to evaluate performance against established objectives have been identified, where suitable and applicable, to improve performance. Management Review meeting minutes describe each objective, the monitoring and/or measurement(s) applied, and the frequency of measurement analysis. The Management Review procedure provides details regarding responsibilities and authorities for reviewing the resulting performance information, for analyzing it, for reacting appropriately, and for reporting QMS performance to employees.

The application of performance monitoring and measurement at two levels reflects the original quality planning that resulted in the development of the QMS in two levels: the process level and the system level. (See 4.2.7, Quality Planning.)

Process Level:

At the process level, attention is focused on ensuring conformity of the product to requirements, and to assure the effectiveness and efficiency of primary processes.

Suitable verification and/or measurements are applied to the product itself to ensure that product conformity has been demonstrated before releasing it to subsequent processing or to the customer. Requirements to perform such verifications appear in procedures where they naturally occur at the appropriate stages in processing. Evidence of conformity with acceptance criteria is maintained as required; such records indicate the person(s) authorizing release. Such verification or measurement is not only an indication of product conformity, but also an indication of the effectiveness of the process to produce planned results. Controls relating to nonconforming product appear in procedures where nonconforming product is encountered.

Suitable monitoring and/or measurement are also applied to each process itself, where applicable. At a minimum, each QMS process is monitored by internal audits, management action, and management review. As determined to be suitable and applicable, further monitoring and measurement of process effectiveness and/or efficiency will be established by top management, including any in-process measurements, as well as those applied to inputs or outputs. Such monitoring or measurement indicators will be identified in Management Review meeting minutes and will be measured, reported, analyzed and acted upon accordingly.

Whenever planned results are not achieved according to results of monitoring or measurement, either at the process or at system level, correction and management actions are taken, as appropriate, to ensure conformity of the product. Process level information is analyzed and acted upon as it arises or becomes available, and periodically according to the discretion of top management. Results are recorded as required. Product release does not proceed until all planned arrangements have been satisfactorily completed, unless otherwise approved by the customer and top management. (Contingency actions are initiated, as applicable.)

System Level:

At the system level, attention is focused on systemic performance—performance of the system of processes in aggregate.

Suitable measurements are applied to the QMS as a whole to evaluate its performance against the quality policy objectives established in Management Review meeting minutes. Internal and external measurements are applied, where feasible. For example, objectives derived from the policy have been established for quality, on-time delivery and customer satisfaction (see below). Appropriate system level information is analyzed and acted upon periodically as required by of Management Review (see the QMS Management procedure), and more frequently as circumstances demand. Results of system level review appear in meeting minutes.

As one measure of QMS performance, customer satisfaction is perhaps the most important. Accordingly, information regarding our customers' perception of our performance is solicited by Customer Satisfaction Surveys according to the Sales procedure, and is analyzed during Management Review according to the QMS Management procedure. Unsolicited feedback, including complaints and returns, is also received, reviewed, and acted upon according to the Sales procedure.

Proficiency with basic statistical techniques is a requirement to hold any management position. (See the Training procedure.) While management personnel use basic statistical techniques as circumstances dictate (e.g. percentages, ratios, averages), no special training is required to apply such techniques. Application of basic statistical techniques is expected in the Sales, Purchasing, Management Action processes and during management review (see the QMS Management procedure), for example. Management of any process is authorized to apply such techniques.

Application of more advanced techniques requires competence as prescribed by the Training procedure. For example, when statistical techniques are applied in connection with determining process or product conformity, including application of sampling plans or SPC, appropriate training is required. Use of more advanced statistical techniques is currently limited to their applications in the Receiving and Production processes, where Quality Control personnel apply a $C = 0$ sampling plan. ($C = 0$ is considered to be validated by the ASQ, from whom it was purchased.) Alternative plans (unless mandated by customers) require validation before use. (Further application and control of statistical techniques is considered during QMS Management meetings.)

4.5. Continual Improvement

Through use of the quality policy, process and system level quality objectives and performance information, audit results, supplier performance analysis, management action and management review, Bob's Machine Shop will continually improve QMS effectiveness and efficiency. (See the QMS Management procedure.)

Improvement is achieved anytime an increased ability to fulfill requirements is demonstrated by measurable results or quantifiable benefits (or estimates thereof).

When opportunities for improvement present themselves by whatever means, management takes advantage of those opportunities by initiating a management action, as appropriate. Improvement efforts may be recorded on Action Forms, and are processed simultaneously with their associated management actions, according to the Management Action procedure. Improvement efforts, like preventive actions, may also be initiated and tracked according to the QMS Management procedure, or during other planning activities.

5. QMS Processes

5.1. Primary Processes

5.1.1. Sales

Generally, the objective of the Sales process is to provide products that will satisfy customers. Inputs include customer requirements, which are normally communicated to the company in the form of Requests for Quotation (RFQs and Purchase Orders (POs). Customer requirements are reviewed to ensure they are clear and complete, and that Bob's Machine Shop has the ability to meet them prior to acceptance. Such requirements also include drawings or specifications bearing product requirements and acceptance criteria.

Sales activities transform the above inputs into their respective outputs: approved Quotations and Sales Orders (residing on the U drive of the company server). Before their approval or acceptance, customers' requirements for product and delivery are verified to be clear and complete, including any requirements that might not have been stated by the customer but are necessary for the proper or safe functioning of the product. The company is verified to have the ability to meet such requirements before orders are accepted and supply is promised.

Based on accepted written orders (verbal orders are not accepted), Travelers are developed and MRP system records to initiate production operations. Travelers bear customers' requirements (and may further reference accompanying drawings or specifications). Another output from Sales is purchasing information relating to infrastructure/resources needed to meet orders' requirements. (These are acquired via the Purchasing process, below.)

Thus, as much of our business consists of repeat business (consisting of the same part numbers), another objective of the Sales process involves production planning, including generation of Travelers used in Production. Any relevant statutory or regulatory requirements or special customer requirements relating to handling, preservation, packaging, delivery, post-delivery, inspection or proposed supply of customer property are also recorded on Travelers. See the Sales procedure.

The Sales procedure also contains provisions for controlling product information, for handling inquiries, for reviewing received orders against any previously agreed requirements or quotations, establishing contingency plans, as well as for reacting to change orders from customers and questions regarding order status.

Inputs to the Sales process also include both solicited and unsolicited feedback regarding the customers' perception of the company's performance, based on the quality and timeliness of the delivered products. The Customer Communications Log serves as the repository for customer communication records. Relevant information is evaluated by management and acted upon appropriately to ensure conformity of product to requirements and to ensure customer satisfaction. Customer satisfaction is measured according to the Management Review procedure, and is reviewed by management accordingly. (Customer satisfaction is measured by satisfaction surveys and by received complaints and returns.)

Where actions are required based on performance information from customers, Action Forms are initiated, as appropriate, and are processed according to the Management Action procedure. (See the Sales procedure.)

5.1.2. Purchasing

Generally, the objective of the Purchasing process is to procure items and services needed to ensure production of quality products. More specifically, the objective of the Purchasing process is to ensure that purchasing information describes needed products and services in requisite detail, that approved orders are submitted to reliable suppliers, and that purchased product is verified to conform to requirements (including customer and/or any regulatory requirements, as well as special processing requirements). Inputs to the Purchasing process include purchasing needs arising in connection with customers' Purchase Orders, purchasing requirements related to maintaining adequate inventory levels, as well as those arising from any QMS process, including Management Review, where resource needs are identified at both the process and system level. (See the Purchasing procedure.)

Potential suppliers may also be viewed as an input to the Purchasing process. Suppliers are evaluated and selected as necessary according to their ability to meet purchasing requirements, and their impact on processing activities and the quality of finished product. Records of supplier approval status appear in the customer database; supplier performance is reviewed during Management Review. Records of review and resulting actions are kept accordingly and are reflected in the supplier list.

Supplier performance is monitored via records of Supplier Incidents. Such records include problems associated with quality, delivery, customer complaints, and returns.

The Purchasing process transforms identified purchasing needs into approved Purchase Orders, which appropriately describe the needed products or services, including requirements for approval or acceptance of the product, as well as any required verification on the suppliers' premises, kan-ban arrangements, or any requirements for the suppliers' QMS, personnel, procedures, processes or equipment (which are not common). Approved Purchase Orders are submitted to approved suppliers, while a copy is retained as an input to the Receiving process, against which incoming products will be verified. (See the Shipping and Receiving procedure, below.)

5.1.3. Shipping and Receiving

Generally, the objective of the Shipping and Receiving process is to ensure that products or services meet applicable requirements before accepting or releasing them, and to prevent damage or deterioration to product during handling and storage. The objective of the Receiving process is to verify incoming products against any applicable requirements, which are contained or referenced by the products' accompanying documentation. Product storage and protection is a mutual objective of Receiving and Shipping. The objective of the Shipping process is to package product to prevent damage during transportation, and releasing product customers.

The Shipping and Receiving procedure describes methods for identifying product with respect to its status (and traceability, where required). Such methods include reference to the products' accompanying documentation, its physical appearance, its location, material labels, etc. The procedure addresses the treatment and use of customer property, as well as preservation methods used during handling, inspection and storage to ensure continuing conformity of product.

Incoming items require receiving inspection to verify
conformity to applicable requirements. Incoming product is
often customer property. Such product is verified through
review of the accompanying documentation against customers
Purchase Orders. Other incoming product is verified against
their associated packing lists and Purchase Orders.

Calibrated devices used to demonstrate conformity to
requirements are controlled according to the Calibration
procedure to ensure the accuracy of the measurements.

Only products passing receiving verification (including
receiving inspection, where required) are accepted, barring
authorized concessions or dispositions. Such product is stored
appropriately while awaiting use. Nonconforming product is
properly identified, evaluated and dispositioned according to
the nonconforming product routine embedded in the Receiving
procedure. Evidence of supplier performance (e.g. quality and
delivery performance) is communicated to Purchasing
personnel using records generated during receiving
verification.

Only product released to Shipping via Production (evidenced
by completed Travelers) is packaged and shipped to customers.
(See the Shipping and Receiving procedure.)

5.1.4. Production

Generally, the objective of the Production process is to produce
quality products (i.e., those meeting applicable requirements)
in a timely manner. More specifically, the objective of the
Production process is to perform realization activities in a
controlled manner to ensure that the resulting product is
effective in meeting requirements. Another objective of the
Production process is to produce quality products as efficiently
as possible. Inputs to the Production process include approved
Travelers and customer blueprints, which specify product
requirements, processing requirements, and any special
customer requirements. Outputs include delivered product that

meets all customer requirements, and completed production records (e.g. completed Travelers and MRP data).

The Production procedure describes methods for identifying product with respect to its inspection status (and traceability, where required). Such methods include reference to the products' accompanying documentation, its physical appearance, its location, color codes, etc. The Production procedure also addresses the treatment and use of customer property, as well as preservation methods used during handling, inspection and storage to ensure continuing conformity of product.

Travelers are created for each production run to contain work instructions needed to produce quality product and verification or inspection requirements and acceptance criteria associated with each processing step. Results of set-up are verified via first piece inspection before operations begin. Verifications demonstrating conformity of product occur at appropriate points during processing according to the Production procedure.

Competent personnel carry out production activities using suitable equipment and according to work instructions to which they have been trained. Product is not released to customers until Travelers are complete and verified. Outputs of the Production process include finished product that meets the acceptance criteria specified by customer blueprints and evidenced by completed Travelers and MRP data. See the Production procedure.

Nonconforming product is properly identified, documented on Travelers, evaluated and dispositioned according to the nonconforming product routine embedded in the Production procedure. Nonconforming product may be scrapped, reworked, or used-as-is, in cases of approved customer deviations or concessions. (Any reworked product is re-verified against the criteria against which it originally failed.) Records of nonconforming product and its disposition are maintained.

Repair maintenance and preventive maintenance is performed as necessary in accordance with the Production procedure. Calibrated devices used during Production to demonstrate conformity to requirements are controlled according to the Calibration procedure.

5.2. Support Processes

5.2.1. Training

Training supports all QMS processes (both primary and support). As a support process, the objective of training is to ensure that competent personnel perform QMS processes (i.e., work that affects quality). Training ensures that competency requirements are identified and that personnel are evaluated and selected based upon the appropriate education, skills, experience and training required for each position affecting quality.

Training is also a mechanism by which the process approach and risk-based thinking is promoted, as is awareness of the quality policy, process and system quality objectives, impact on QMS performance, and consequences of failing to follow procedures.

Training is provided as needed, the effectiveness of which is evaluated to verify competence before assigning work. A Training Record exists for each employee to demonstrate that employee's competence to perform assigned work. Training Records also identify where further training needs have been identified for employees, as applicable. A training matrix identifies process-specific competencies. See the Training procedure.

5.2.2. Document and Record Control

Document and Record Control supports all QMS processes. As a support process, the objective of document control is to ensure that legible, approved documentation is available to employees when and where it is needed in order to perform process activities correctly. The procedure describes how such documentation is initially approved and how it is re-approved after being updated, and how the most current version of any QMS documentation is determined. The procedure also describes treatment of documents originating externally.

Document Control ensures that only approved, current, controlled documentation is used, and that obsolete documentation is removed from use.

The objective of Record Control is to ensure that records of processing activities are maintained as long as they are useful. Such records demonstrate the effective operation of the QMS and conformity to applicable requirements (including any specified by customers and/or by regulatory agencies). The President establishes retention periods. Record Control ensures that quality records are appropriately stored to be protected from theft, damage and deterioration, that they are readily identifiable and retrievable when they are needed, and that they are disposed of properly once their usefulness has expired. The Record Retention Form specifies responsibilities for maintaining records, their storage and protection, their retrieval or filing method, their retention periods and their method of disposal. Where customers specify retention requirements, associated records are listed on the Record Retention Form and are retained accordingly. (See the Document and Record Control procedure.)

5.2.3. Management Action

Management Action supports all QMS processes and improvement activities. As a support process, the objective of the Management Action process is to identify systemic or process-related problems or undesirable situations, or the potential thereof, to determine the cause(s), and to take action to address those causes or risks so that they do not recur, or preferably, to prevent them from arising in the first place.

Requests for management action are processed using an Action Form, each of which is tracked using the Action Log. Once closed, Action Forms provide evidence of actions taken and verification of their effectiveness, while closure is also recorded in the Action Log.

Appropriate actions are taken to eliminate the causes of existing problems or nonconformities in order to prevent their recurrence. Error-proofing methods are employed wherever applicable. Actions are taken in response to information arising from audit results, customer feedback or complaints, supplier performance data, performance information regarding product nonconformity, process monitoring and measurement results, etc. Actions also arise in connection with improvement efforts associated with any QMS process or source of information.

According to the Management Action procedure, the following steps are taken for each Management Action initiated: the problem is reviewed and its cause(s) determined using appropriate problem-solving methods; possible actions to eliminate its root cause to prevent its recurrence are evaluated and an appropriate action is selected and implemented; records of the completed action are maintained; the effectiveness of the action taken is verified.

Appropriate actions are also taken to eliminate the causes of potential nonconformities or undesirable situations in order to prevent their occurrence. These actions are taken preemptively in response to the same information sources as corrective-type actions (above), in addition to unforeseeable external information, when the information suggests that potential for a problem exists, or that a problem is likely, presenting a risk to achieving quality objectives.

Whenever Management Action is taken, consideration is given to applying the action to other similar circumstances or areas in order to prevent the problem from arising in those other areas, wherever possible. Any risks or opportunities identified during previous planning are updated, as necessary.

According to the Management Action procedure, the following steps are taken when risks to quality present themselves: the issue is reviewed and its cause(s) or potential impact(s) are determined; containment planning is conducted, as appropriate; possible actions to solve the problem are evaluated; an appropriate action is selected and implemented; records of the completed action are maintained; the effectiveness of the action taken is verified.

Should actions prove ineffective, alternative solutions will be evaluated and applied until the issue is resolved. (See the Management Action procedure.)

5.2.4. Internal Audits

Internal Audits support all QMS processes. As a support process, the objective of Internal Audits is to monitor processing activities at planned intervals to ensure their effective implementation and upkeep, to ensure that they comply with the planned arrangements described by QMS documentation, and to confirm their continuing compliance with the requirements of ISO 9001:2008.

Internal Audits verify that working practice is conducted in accordance with the quality policy, procedures, and provisions in this manual, ensuring that issues regarding compliance are resolved appropriately. All QMS processes are audited internally. Internal Audits are scheduled according to the status and importance of the activities being audited according to the requirements of the Audit Schedule. Qualified Internal Auditors conduct internal audits according to the instructions, scope, criteria and any specific methods appearing on Audit Report forms. (Alternatively, qualified contracted personnel may conduct internal audits. See the Internal Audits procedure.)

Where working practice fails to conform to planned arrangements, or when problems or opportunities for improvement are discovered, auditors generate findings, which are recorded on Action Forms.

Upon completion of an audit, auditors summarize their findings and conclusions on the associated Audit Report form, and submit the report and findings to management, who take timely action. Action Forms arising from audits will be processed according to the Management Action procedure to ensure that effective action is taken in a timely manner. Internal Audits are conducted, reported and the results acted upon according to the Internal Audits, Management Action and QMS Management Review procedures.

5.2.5. Calibration

Calibration supports the Receiving and Production processes. In support of these processes, the objective of Calibration is to ensure that suitable, accurate measuring equipment is used to demonstrate conformity of product to applicable requirements. The Calibration process ensures that measuring devices are selected and used in a manner consistent with measuring requirements, and that such devices are calibrated or verified periodically (or before use) to ensure their continuing fitness for use, in order to impart confidence that the devices are suitable in their precision and that the resulting measurements are accurate.

The Calibration procedure ensures that calibration results bear traceability to international or national standards. The procedure also ensures that such devices are appropriately identified, handled, stored and safeguarded to prevent damage and deterioration. Routine calibrations are conducted according to schedule, while results and historical performance data are recorded in each device's Calibration Record. Verification of devices before use is logged in the Calibrate Before Use log. Should any monitoring or measurement software be introduced to the QMS, it will be treated as a calibrated device and will be confirmed and reconfirmed as necessary to ensure its continuing suitability.

When a device is found to be out of calibration, the Quality Manager will investigate the impact of the potentially errant measurements on product previously measured with the device to ensure that the impact is known, that it is corrected or otherwise resolved, and that all affected parties are notified, as appropriate. Unsuitable devices are withdrawn from use, or their use is limited to be appropriate for the measurements being carried out. See the Calibration procedure.

5.2.6. QMS Management

The QMS Management procedure describes management of the QMS, including how performance data from various sources is analyzed and acted upon, including information relating to customer satisfaction, quality (i.e. conformance to requirements), process or product performance trends suggesting need for improvement or preventive action, and supplier performance. Such measurements are analyzed and acted upon in an effort to improve performance. The procedure also describes periodic consideration of applying further statistical techniques to control process variability, to control product characteristics, or to further analyze performance data.

Inputs to Management Review meetings include audit results, customer feedback, information regarding effectiveness of previous management actions in addressing risks and opportunities, supplier performance information, internal performance information regarding product conformity and process monitoring and measurement, any identified improvement opportunities or recommendations, and any identified internal or external changes that could impact the QMS. (See the Management Review Agenda and Minutes.)

Top management periodically reviews the QMS as a whole to determine its effectiveness in meeting objectives and applicable requirements, including those of our customers and those of ISO 9001:2008. This review also includes evaluation of the cost of poor quality (via rework time and returned product). Top management also determines whether the QMS, the quality policy and quality objectives are still suitable and adequate for the company, according to the Management Review Agenda and Minutes, which when complete, stands as the record of review. Where actions are required based on information from whatever source, Action Forms are initiated, as appropriate, and are processed according to the Management Action procedure. (See the QMS Management procedure.)

Once performance levels are analyzed and QMS effectiveness has been determined, performance information is communicated to employees, so they understand how their performance affects the achievement of established objectives. Such communication occurs through verbal reporting during meetings or on an individual basis. Performance results may also be posted in a conspicuous location.

6. Change History

Original issue: 09/13/95

Generally re-written to meet requirements of ISO 9001:2000: 09/15/00

Generally re-written to describe the QMS and processes (complying with ISO 9001:2015): 01/15/16

Implications for Auditing

The Logical Principle of Transitivity and QMS Auditing

In a perfect world, it seems QMS assessment should resemble, at some level, the logical principle of transitivity. If $a = b$ and $b = c$, then $a = c$. Here's how this works in the context of QMS assessment. We'll set up a, b and c below to illustrate the point.

> a) ISO 9001 requirements
> b) Planned arrangements (captured in documented procedures)
> c) Working practice

If b conforms to a, and c conforms to b, then c conforms to a. In other words, if the documentation conforms to the standard, and working practices conform to the documentation, then the QMS conforms to the standard.

At Stage 1, the question is, "Is the story good?" In other words, do the planned arrangements meet requirements? From an auditee's perspective, "Does what we say we do meet requirements?"

At Stage 2, the question becomes, "Is the story true?" Or, given the acceptability of the planned arrangements established during Stage 1, does working practice comply with those planned arrangements? From an auditee's perspective, the question is, "Do we do what we say we do?"

The Problem with Standard-Based Audits

Sometime after the release of ISO 9001:2000, a shortcoming of ISO 9001 auditing became clear: CB auditors were often using a standard-based approach to auditing. Auditors would arrive at an audit client's worksite armed with a copy of ISO 9001 as a Stage 2 audit checklist. This appeared to allow inconsistent application of the requirements.

In the midst of this prevailing mindset, the ostensible shortcoming was this: using a single copy of the requirements as audit criteria, parts of a quality management system (QMS) are not assessed. Once conformity to a requirement is found, other areas where the requirement applies are not assessed for conformity to that requirement.

For example, if an auditor arrives at a manufacturing company armed with a checklist consisting of the standard's requirements, the trouble starts when assessing realization processes. Let's say the next blank check-boxes appearing on a standard-based checklist contain the product identification requirements. The auditor's current mission is to verify conformity to those requirements. So, the auditor goes into, say, the receiving area. There, the auditor finds conformity to the product identification requirements. The auditor duly ticks the check-box. Conformity verified. Good job. Next check-box.

But when the auditor proceeds to manufacturing processes, say, an assembly process, the product identification requirements are no longer at issue. Why? Those check-boxes have already been ticked. The system has already demonstrated conformity to this requirement during this audit. So processes to which requirements pertain were not consistently being assessed to those requirements.

The answer to this problem, reasons a standard-based mindset, is to determine which ISO 9001 requirements pertain to which QMS processes. Then, be sure to have enough copies of the relevant requirements to apply them to each process to which they pertain during Stage 2. So, if it was determined that, say, four processes encountered product in need of identification, then Stage 1 audit preparation involved developing standard-based checklists for each of those four processes. Can you see how complicated this is starting to become?

Each checklist would include a copy of the product identification requirements (among others). That way, the product identification requirements would be addressed in an audit of each of those four processes. This was regarded as a process audit, thought to represent the "process approach to auditing." This does not represent a true process approach to auditing. This solution simply represents a more thorough standard-based approach to auditing. The Stage 2 auditor under this arrangement is still left assessing conformity directly to ISO

9001 requirements at Stage 2. The fundamental problem has not changed at all.

When management's planned arrangements are not documented or known to a Stage 1 auditor, as is commonly the case, it is the auditor's job at Stage 2 to determine what those arrangements are. Right there on the spot, "good" standard-based Stage 2 auditing requires auditors to determine what planned arrangements are in order to assess conformity to them.

Stage 1 Audits

QMS auditing begins with determining how an organization addresses applicable requirements during Stage 1 auditing. Also during Stage 1, working documents such as audit checklists are developed for use during Stage 2.

A checklist resulting from a process approach to auditing is composed of questions unique to each audit, specific to each organization and to each process. Using a standard-based approach, a pre-written checklist is used, echoing the same mistake as using a standard-based approach to implementing a QMS.

If a QMS has not demonstrated a process approach, this should be identified during Stage 1, when a review of QMS documents is performed. Stage 2 should not proceed until there is a satisfactory Stage 1 result.

Process-based auditing places appropriate emphasis on the importance of the Stage 1 audit. Proper application of the standard and its requirements presupposes a process approach to QMS implementation. Regardless of audit approach, however, if QMSs are undefined or ill-defined by a standard-based approach, conformity assessment is compromised in Stage 2.

Remember the conformity matrix showing which processes are responsible for complying with which specific requirements. Such a matrix reveals to an auditor which requirements to focus upon during the audit of a given process. (Accuracy of such matrices should also be verified during Stage 1.)

However, simply collecting the requirements applicable to a given process and auditing to those requirements during Stage 2 is problematic. This standard-based approach assesses conformity only to requirements, but not necessarily to the organization's plans, or, planned arrangements. If planned arrangements meeting realization requirements are not defined, as is the case using a six-element approach, objectively assessing conformity to planned arrangements seems impossible during Stage 2.

If a conformity audit proceeds to Stage 2 without these planned arrangements being known through objective documented Stage 1 evidence, it appears to be the auditor's responsibility to determine management's planned arrangements by examining working practice on-site during Stage 2. This creates wide potential for error, because the assessment process is now subject to the auditor's interpretation of what management's planned arrangements are.

Once auditors believe that they understand planned arrangements based on their subjective observations, they are then responsible for assessing if working practice conforms to the planned arrangements. While consistency can be confirmed to some degree in this scenario during a single audit, there can be no confidence that this consistency will stay in place over time. While consistency may be desirable, it doesn't demonstrate conformity to best practices defined by management. So, it could be that a process is being done consistently wrong. Or, not being defined, maybe it was consistent on that day, but it changes every day.

During Stage 1, an assessor reviews QMS documents to assess conformity to ISO 9001 requirements. Since 2000, conformity to applicable requirements is arguably no longer required of documented QMS procedures. However, failure to document planned arrangements for proper processing poses a risk to consistent processing and the viable assessment of conformity.

If conformity to applicable requirements is not defined by an organization's QMS documentation (even if a process approach was used), it seems appropriate to raise a finding during Stage 1. Such a finding might be worded thus: "This lack of definition and procedural support poses a risk to consistent processing, consistent application of best practices, and to the assessment of process conformity." The objective of a Stage 1 audit is not to verify that procedures say what the standard says, rather, it's to assess whether stated planned arrangements comply with what the standard says.

Once conformity of planned arrangements to applicable requirements is clear at Stage 1, the auditor should record this evidence of conformity in each case for later verification during Stage 2. It could be added to a process-based audit checklist—be sure to use organizational language from the procedure itself. Or, the procedural provisions suggesting conformity could simply be highlighted in the procedure itself (noting which requirement is addressed) to serve as a checklist. Either way, using a process-based checklist, the audit criteria for Stage 2 is couched in the organization's terms, not in terms of the standard. (Audit schedules currently often properly allow for auditor preparation time, presumably enough time to develop process-based checklists for each process-based audit.)

Using the process approach to auditing, Stage 2 audits are more process-centric than ISO-centric. With the "ISOese" language barrier out of the way, audits are more effective. Process audits are properly focused on determining conformity to organizations' procedures (reflecting planned arrangements) and at the same time confirming conformity to the requirements of the standard.

Auditors should be checking, at Stage 2, that working practice complies with management's planned arrangements (or, the "organization's own requirements"--ISO 9001, 2008, 0.1, or ". . . the organization's own requirements for its quality management system" per ISO 9001:2015, 9.2.1a).

These arrangements must be documented somehow in order for a Stage 1 auditor to assess whether these arrangements meet ISO 9001 requirements. That's part of the objective of a Stage 1 audit: to ensure that adequate process documentation exists, and that it clearly defines management's planned arrangements.

Proceeding with a Stage 2 audit without a successful Stage 1 audit only compromises audit results. The Stage 2 audit would be conducted without any audit criteria being defined. If these arrangements were not clear at Stage 1, it is unethical to proceed to Stage 2. (Unfortunately, it is also common.)

It's easy enough to pull the wool over an auditor's eyes. And now the auditor must rely on the auditees at hand to convey what management's planned arrangements are—by showing what they are doing and how they do it. For example, an auditor might observe line workers making ball bearings on an assembly line. From this observation alone, the auditor would be responsible to determine if the ball bearings are being made the way management says they should be made. With no documentation defining how the process is supposed to work, the auditor must rely on whatever the line workers say.

When planned arrangements are not documented, there is no objective standard against which to assess working practices. It's easy to come up with a story to fit the evidence on audit day, and it's also easy to agree to it the day before in preparation for the audit. If management's planned arrangements are not consistently defined somehow, how can a Stage 2 audit conclude that working practice complies with planned arrangements?

Process-Centric Stage 2 Audits

The focus of the audit at Stage 2 should be conformity to planned arrangements. Again, auditors should be verifying, at Stage 2, that working practice complies with management's planned arrangements.

If, at Stage 1, planned arrangements were already confirmed to meet the requirements of the standard, Stage 2 now focuses upon whether working practice complies with those planned arrangements. Stage 2 should determine if these planned arrangements are being consistently followed by those performing work affecting quality.

Results of a process audit reveal information about process performance, thereby offering more value to management. These results indicate not merely conformity to requirements, but conformity to management's planned arrangements—however these arrangements have been defined.

Example: Bob's Machine Shop

The Calibration process at Bob's has been in place since Bob started doing commercial work. It is documented in process fashion.

An auditor using a standard-based approach arrived for the Stage 2 audit armed with the pertinent requirements of ISO 9001:2008, clause 7.6, Control of monitoring and measuring equipment. As the standard does not explicitly require a documented procedure here, processing requirements pertaining to calibration activities (described by Bob's Calibration procedure) are unknown to an auditor focused only upon the "six required" procedures.

The auditor asked auditees questions based upon the standard, often couched in "ISOese:"

"How do you . . .

- "Calibrate or verify, 'or both, at specified intervals, or prior to use . . . '?" (ISO 9001:2008, 7.6 a.)

- "Identify 'equipment needed to provide evidence of conformity of product to determined requirements'?" (ISO 9001:2008, 7.6. general and c)

- "Safeguard equipment 'from adjustments that would invalidate' results'?" (ISO 9001:2008, 7.6 d.)

Auditees should not be expected to know ISO 9001 requirements, unless they are internal auditors. Auditees are supposed to know their procedures and they are supposed to be demonstrably following those procedures. Questions couched in "ISOese" needlessly confuse personnel. However, even when auditors using a standard-based approach rely less upon "ISOese," they cannot escape the standard-based audit plan they have effectively implemented. They are auditing to ISO 9001 requirements, not to the organization's internal processing requirements complying with ISO 9001 requirements.

The Process Approach to Auditing Bob's Machine Shop

Conversely, an auditor using a process approach arrives and says to Bob, "I understand that you are using the old index card routine that was common in the military for years. That should work fine; it's a very simple and effective method. Let's have a look at the index card file . . ."

Stage 2 of a process-based audit assumes the process was adequately vetted against ISO 9001 requirements during Stage 1. Some kind of documentation must be available to Stage 1 auditors to show that the organization's processing requirements satisfy requirements of the standard. In Bob's case, he supplied his Calibration procedure, which describes his planned arrangements for controlling calibration activities and calibrated devices. During Stage 1, the auditor reviewed these planned arrangements against the requirements of 7.6 (ISO 9001:2008 or 7.1.5 of ISO 9001:2015) and found them to be acceptable in meeting requirements.

The purpose of Stage 2 is now to determine if these planned arrangements have been effectively implemented. That means, determine if the process is being performed as planned, while producing expected results.

So, the auditor here asks questions arising from Bob's own Calibration procedure. Using a process approach to auditing, checklists are unique to each audit of each process. (Process audits do not use pre-written checklists based upon the standard, nor pre-written checklists based upon something other than the defined process at hand.)

Knowing the procedure (or, having a checklist based upon the procedure itself), the process-based auditor is "smart." She fundamentally knows the answer to every question she asks before she asks it. She is not asking questions about proper process performance because she doesn't know the answer, as her standard-based counterpart must.

She might not need to ask as many questions, either. She already knows from Bob's Calibration procedure that all devices under calibration control are identified with calibration stickers, except for ring gages and thread gages. Stickers won't stick on these items very well, so they are identified by unique "Cal ID" numbers engraved on a noncritical surface of each such gage. Cal ID numbers enable calibration status to be determined by accessing respective index cards in the index card file.

Aware of this, the auditor might request, "Show me your thread gage collection." Knowing the procedure, she knows what she wants to see and why she wants to see it. She looks at some thread gages, jots down some numbers, and checks them against the index cards. She knows conformity when she sees it.

Management should be more interested in the results of a process-based audit than they are in the results of a standard-based audit. Process-based audits tell them something about their operations, not merely about conformity to ISO 9001. If operations don't follow the plan, of what value is the plan? Why apply process measures and take action to improve a plan if the plan isn't consistently followed in the first place? Because they assess conformity to management's planned arrangements, audits using a process approach provide more value to management.

Take Back Your Quality Management System

A Process Approach is Required

A process approach is not just a good idea anymore. It's required. ISO 9001:2000 required a process approach, but this requirement was often overlooked. ISO 9001:2008 provided more teeth to make the process approach more enforceable. For example, the 2008 revision closed an apparent loophole that had allowed a disparity between the letter and the intent of the year 2000 requirements. 4.1a) of the year 2000 requirements required organizations to "identify processes needed for the quality management system and their application throughout the organization . . ." (italics added). The 2008 revision requires organizations to "determine the processes needed for the quality management system . . ." (italics added).

What's the difference between "identify" and "determine"? Used elsewhere in the standard, the word "identify" could be taken to mean, basically, "label," as in the "product identification" requirement. So, organizations using a standard-based approach could comply with the letter of ISO 9001:2000, 4.1 a) by labeling QMS processes any way they like.

While labeling processes according to the elements of the standard meets the letter of the requirement, it stands in stark contrast to the endorsement of a process approach at 0.2 Process approach. It also conflicts with a sentence appearing in the preceding section, ISO 9001:2000, 0.1: "It is not the intent of this International Standard to imply uniformity in the structure of quality management systems or uniformity of documentation."

Who uses uniformly structured systems and documentation? The answer is every organization using a standard-based approach. There are enough of these organizations to warrant an express statement by the standard's authors.

The Process Approach of ISO 9001

On the other hand, ISO 9001:2008, 4.1 a) requires organizations to "determine" QMS processes. Used elsewhere in ISO 9001, the word "determine" involves investigation to arrive at certainty, as in the requirements to determine customer requirements or to determine the root causes of systemic problems. So simply identifying processes is no longer adequate. (If it were, this word would not have been changed.)

Determining organizational processes or departments shouldn't be a difficult task, but getting it wrong (i.e., using a standard-based approach) will foil proper interpretation and application of several following requirements. That's one reason why the standard demands a process approach.

In ISO 9001:2008 (like ISO 9001:2000), the requirements needed to assess application of a process approach mostly reside in 4.1, General requirements. From ISO 9001:2008, 4.1:

"4.1 General requirements

The organization shall establish, document, implement and maintain a quality management system and continually improve its effectiveness in accordance with the requirements of this International Standard.

The organization shall

a) determine the processes needed for the quality management system and their application throughout the organization (see 1.2),

b) determine the sequence and interaction of these processes,

c) determine criteria and methods needed to ensure that both the operation and control of these processes are effective,

d) ensure the availability of resources and information necessary to support the operation and monitoring of these processes,

e) monitor, measure where applicable, and analyze these processes, and

f) implement actions necessary to achieve planned results and continual improvement of these processes.

These processes shall be managed by the organization in accordance with the requirements of this International Standard."

Notice that the word "process" appears prominently in each sentence of 4.1. The processes in question, of course, are core processes and support processes needed for a (quality) management system.

ISO 9001:2015 provides even more visibility to the process approach requirement.

The process approach was already required of ISO 9001:2008, but section 4.4 of the new standard will make this more "explicit." It's not new, it's being clarified. Notice that the language of ISO 9001:2015 at 4.4 (below) closely resembles the language contained above in ISO 9001:2008, 4.1.

From ISO 9001:2015, 4.4:

"The organization shall establish, implement, maintain and continually improve a quality management system, including the processes needed and their interactions, in accordance with the requirements of this International Standard.

The organization shall determine the processes needed for the quality management system and their application throughout the organization, and shall:

a) determine the inputs required and the outputs expected from these processes;

b) determine the sequence and interaction of these processes;

c) determine and apply the criteria and methods (including monitoring, measurements and related performance indicators) needed to ensure the effective operation and control of these processes;

d) determine the resources needed for these processes and

ensure their availability;

e) assign the responsibilities and authorities for these processes;

f) address the risks and opportunities as determined in accordance with the requirements of 6.1;

g) evaluate these processes and implement any changes needed to ensure that these processes achieve their intended results;

h) improve the processes and the quality management system.

The organization shall maintain documented information to the extent necessary to support the operation of processes and retain documented information to the extent necessary to have confidence that the processes are being carried out as planned."

Notice how closely a) – h) of the 2015 standard resembles a) – f) of the 2008 standard. In the 2015 standard, a) – h) are more clearly cast to elaborate upon what is meant by applying a process approach. They provide an auditor with the means to determine if a process approach has been applied.

The standard provides a basis for nonconformities to be raised against QMSs that fail to demonstrate a process approach. A standard-based approach fails to demonstrate conformity with the requirements of ISO 9001:2008 and ISO 900:2015. The following is one example of a finding against a QMS demonstrating a standard-based approach. Let's go back to Bob's Machine's QMS, before the suggestion to adopt the process approach. (Note that real-life findings are not as lengthy and detailed as the examples provided.)

REQUIREMENT: ISO 9001:2015, 4.4.1 states that, "The organization shall determine the processes needed for the quality management system and their application throughout the organization, and shall a) determine the inputs required and the outputs expected from these processes . . ."

EVIDENCE: During Stage 1 assessment, the organization's operational processes were found to be: Sales, Purchasing, Receiving, Production, and Shipping. However, the QMS is defined as including or being composed of the following operational processes (see the Quality Manual, rev A, clause 1.2.3, and the referenced QMS procedures): Quality System, Identification and Traceability, Process Control, Customer Property, Inspection and Test, Inspection and Test Status, Preservation of Product, and Statistical Techniques.

The provided QMS documentation does not demonstrate that the processes needed for the quality management system have been determined (and supported by documented information pursuant to ISO 9001:2015 4.4.2). Although the Contract Review procedure specifies how some Sales processes are carried out, and the *Purchasing* procedure describes the Purchasing process, the balance of the documented procedures do not address requirements in process fashion for the remaining operational processes: Receiving, Production, and Shipping.

Contrary to ISO 9001:2015, 4.4.1a), the inputs and outputs expected of the defined QMS processes (e.g., "Customer Property" or "Inspection and Test Status") are not the inputs and outputs required of operational processes (e.g., Receiving or Production); moreover, these processes cannot be sequenced to result in the output of product, contrary to ISO 9001:2015 4.4.1b).

By dedicating procedures to requirements rather than (or in addition to) dedicating them to processes, the system structure and documentation demonstrates confusion between requirements and processes needed for the quality management system. As a result of treating requirements as if they were processes—by dedicating procedures to them—processes are procedurally confused with, for example, activities, methods, customer property, and statistical techniques.

c) <u>NONCONFORMITY</u>: In failing to effectively determine the processes needed for the quality management system—by excluding processes affecting quality from the system (i.e., Production, Receiving, and Shipping)—while identifying and documenting the standard's requirements as being processes needed for the management system instead) the organization has not met the requirements of ISO 9001:2015, 4.4.1: "The organization shall determine the processes needed for the quality management system and their application throughout the organization . . ."

(Please refer to ISO/TC 176/SC 2/N525R2, Introduction and support package: Guidance on the documentation requirements of ISO 9001:2008, and ISO/TC 176/SC 2/N544R3, ISO 9000 Introduction and Support Package: Guidance on the Concept and Use of the Process Approach for management systems. Also refer to ISO 9000:2015, for information about the process approach and for the definitions of "process" and "procedure.")

Despite widespread confusion between the standard-based approach and the process approach, precious little information is available from ISO regarding the distinction between the two. Official guidance, which is updated and improved every now and then, includes:

- "An organization that has not used a process approach in the past will need to pay particular attention to the definition of its processes, their sequence and interaction."

- "It is stressed that ISO 9001 requires (and always has required) a 'Documented quality management system', and not a 'system of documents'."—ISO/TC 176/SC 2/N525R2, Introduction and support package: Guidance on the documentation requirements of ISO 9001:2008, October, 2008 (http://www.iso.org/iso/iso_catalogue/management_standards),

- "All processes should be aligned with the objectives, scope and complexity of the organization, and should be designed to add value to the organization."

- ". . . Each organization should define the number and type of processes needed to fulfill its business objectives. It is permissible for a process that is required by ISO 9001:2008 to be part of a process (or processes) that is already established by the organization, or to be defined by the organization in terms that are different to those in ISO 9001." —ISO/TC 176/SC 2/N544R3, ISO 9000 Introduction and Support Package: Guidance on the Concept and Use of the Process Approach for management systems, October, 2008 [Caveat: this guidance appears to mix the explanation of a process approach with that of a system approach.] (http://www.iso.org/iso/iso_catalogue/management_standards),

- "If the auditor considers this as the right approach [. . . each clause or sub-clause of ISO 9001 be defined as a separate process . . .], he should refer to relevant ISO documents . . . which clearly indicates the contrary." –ISO/IAF ISO 9001 Auditing Practices Group Guidance on: Identification of Processes, June 5, 2009 (http://isotc.iso.org/), and

- "Helping an auditor to interpret the process approach. . . If an auditor does not understand or misunderstands the process approach, direct him or her to recognized information sources . . ."

   "A certification body should ensure that all its auditors have received sufficient training regarding the requirements in ISO 9001, particularly those on the process approach." –ISO/IAF ISO 9001 Auditing Practices Group Guidance on: Understanding the process approach, June 5, 2009. (http://isotc.iso.org/).

In addition to standards and guidance documents, ISO also publishes a magazine called *ISO Management Systems* (IMS). As to whether ISO

The Process Approach of ISO 9001

9001 actually requires a process approach, one issue of IMS speaks directly to this question. And the answer is succinct: "ISO 9001 requires a process approach." See ISO Management Systems, November-December 2009, special report column: "MSS+ Management systems need more than just management system standards" © ISO Management Systems (http://www.iso.org/ims).

The argument against a standard-based approach is clear:

1) The standard requires a process approach,

2) A standard-based approach does not demonstrate a process approach (and instead contradicts it), so

3) A standard-based approach does not demonstrate conformity to the standard.

Notice that this argument holds true for organizations registered to sector schemes of ISO 9001 as well.

The Value of ISO 9001

Dissatisfaction with the value provided by ISO 9001 generally to arises in part from misplaced expectations arising in part due to a misunderstanding of the standard.

Generally, the intent of ISO 9001 is to reduce risk associated with doing business with unknown suppliers in a global economy. The idea is to provide a set of criteria against which QMSs across the globe can be evenly assessed. It's a tool to determine if organizations have systems in place to deliver whatever it promises (as opposed to merely being good at making promises). In theory, if you know nothing else about a potential supplier in, say, Bangladesh, except the organization is ISO 9001 certified, you know that a system is in place to consistently deliver quality product, and that customer satisfaction is a priority of this potential supplier. They are not just a "fly-by-night" or "don't-really-know-how-to-do-it" type of organization. To be certified, an organization (in theory) must demonstrate that it has a planned system in operation.

Think of ISO 9001 like a high school examination, like a biology test. What is being tested is an organization's QMS and its ability to deliver. It's a basic two-part question: "Does the defined QMS effectively satisfy the requirements of ISO 9001?" (Stage 1 auditing), and, "Is that defined system effectively implemented?" (Stage 2 auditing). If the answer to both parts of the question is in the affirmative, the organization passes the test. If not, some further work is needed on the organization's part to pass the test.

Although the organization pays auditors who arrive on-site to conduct Stage 2 auditing, the auditors don't work for the organization in a sense that many have come to expect. Think of the auditor as someone administering the test, an exam proctor. The proctor isn't there to help anyone pass the test. The proctor is there simply to administer the test and should not be expected to add tremendous value beyond that.

The auditor is not there with the primary intention of fixing or improving your operations, the auditor is merely trying to determine if the system passes the test. The auditor represents not only your customers, but potential customers all over the world. Again, it is not within the auditor's purview to help you pass your audit; the auditor's loyalty should be to the standard and its intent. Technically, the auditor should be disinterested as to whether an auditee passes or not; the auditor is there simply to administer the test and objectively determine if you pass or not.

Contrary to popular belief, ISO auditors are not necessarily quality management experts—and the standard does not assert that they need to be. An auditor possesses the requisite expertise with ISO 9001 to effectively apply it as audit criteria. Just because the auditor can administer the test, it doesn't follow that the auditor can tell you how to run or improve your operations.

While it's true that in the course of auditing, auditors may identify opportunities for improvement, and this is within their purview, their primary concern is assessing the system for effectiveness and conformity. Sure, while auditing, an auditor might notice things that people working in the processes every day just wouldn't notice. An auditor aware of common best practices might skillfully impart these during audits. However, auditors aren't supposed to consult. They're not supposed to advise audit clients about how best to meet ISO 9001 requirements. In fact, it's not ethical for an auditor to consult an audit client in this manner during an audit.

So while it's possible for auditors to identify opportunities for improvement, management should not expect ISO 9001 auditors to coach them on how to improve their systems or how to best handle ISO 9001 requirements. It's an unfair expectation. It's unfair to auditors. It pressures them to consult. Furthermore, it sets them up for failure when, contrary to expectations, their audit reports fail to provide management with useful advice for meeting requirements or sage guidance for improving operations.

It is, and always was, management's job to improve the business and how it operates. The essential part of an auditor's job—the reason for auditing—is to draw a conclusion regarding whether or not a system passes the test.

So, where's the value?

Management should find value in the systematic output of quality product every day. Of course, management already sees the value in that. Each system of value-adding processes provides the context of its QMS. The QMS is an endoskeleton residing within those processes, not an exoskeleton imposed upon them. Integrated into processing, management should find value in a QMS designed for results, one designed to improve performance of their operations. Quality good or bad is naturally built into processing, as are QMSs.

Once the process approach is understood, the standard doesn't represent a framework for management. The QMS represents a framework for management. Then, much of ISO 9001 can be viewed as a listing of known mistakes to avoid or known risks to control, things to consider when developing a management framework.

Representing quality professionals from all over the world, the authors of the standard are familiar with common quality problems and their sources. For example, if you don't identify product during processing, you're likely to have quality problems. If you use uncontrolled documents in operations, you are likely to have quality problems. Or, if you employ incompetent personnel to conduct operations, you are likely to have quality problems. The standard requires control over these known sources of risk to quality.

It seems only right that an international standard for quality assurance would include requirements to control these known sources of risk to quality. Successful organizations controlled these risks for years before ISO 9001 came along.

Now embedded in ISO 9001 requirements, management of organizations seeking certification needs to take these sources of risk into account when planning internal processing requirements. So sure, management can glean information about quality system development from examining the requirements against which QMSs are assessed. It's only prudent. Examining requirements might also help understand the degree to which a system needs to be developed to pass minimum international muster. So ISO 9001 can be used to self-assess planned arrangements.

However, ISO 9001 requirements apply to defined systems; they are not intended to define those systems. With this understanding, management can use ISO 9001 while developing a QMS—merely being mindful of ISO 9001 requirements while defining their own operations, without allowing ISO 9001 requirements to define their own operations.

Quality management is far too wide and varied for an international standard to define it for everyone. The intention of ISO 9001 was never to tell the world how to manage quality. So, beyond promoting PDCA, ISO 9001 doesn't define quality management for anyone. ISO 9001 (or procedures based on ISO 9001) cannot effectively define or describe how to manage quality in any organization's operations. Management does that.

The Process Approach of ISO 9001

Those looking for value in ISO 9001 as a guide for managing quality or structuring QMSs are simply looking in the wrong place. While ISO 9001 clearly contains QMS requirements, these requirements are intended to promote uniform QMS assessment, not to promote uniform quality management or uniform QMSs.

Once released from the expectation that ISO 9001 tells organizations how to manage quality, ISO 9001 seems to derive its value from two sources. First, it offers value to the purchasing function as a supplier selection device—consistent with its original intent. Second, beyond the requirement to do business with some customers, it adds value to the sales and marketing functions of certified organizations. Certification suggests to potential customers that you have a system in place to meet their requirements—so you are serious about satisfying them.

ISO Made Easy

Although one intention of ISO 9001 has always been to promote best practices in quality assurance, it's fair to say that the opportunity for improvement in this regard is substantial. More than just a few registered QMSs employ a standard-based approach. The failure of many QMS implementations is largely due to poor quality concepts arising from a popular but bad idea about how ISO 9001 is applied and what it requires. But your company doesn't need to suffer through it any longer. Organizational management is largely in control of organizations' experience with quality management and ISO 9001.

Put some quality into your quality system: adopt a process approach. Your company will save time and money, and personnel from all areas and levels of your organization will thank you. Most importantly, you will be left with a sensible system that can be understood and driven by management.

Once core processes are determined, the requirements ISO 9001:2008, 4.1 (General requirements) seem much more sensible, as do the requirements of section 7 (Production realization). Knowing which processes the standard is referring to—the ones really needed for a QMS—the temptation to search the standard for 'realization processes' is gone.

QMS documentation is then developed in support of real QMS processes. While there is much more to the process approach than documentation, poor QMS documentation based upon the standard will stymie proper process and system definition from the outset.

ISO 9001:2008 4.1a) requires that processes needed for the QMS are determined; b) requires that the sequence and interaction of these QMS processes is determined; c) requires that criteria needed to ensure the effective operation and control of these QMS processes is determined; d) requires that the appropriate resources are available to support operation of these QMS processes, e) requires QMS processes to be at least monitored, if not measured, for performance analysis; and f) requires actions to be taken in order to achieve results as planned and to improve these QMS processes. The standard then requires these QMS processes to be managed in accordance with the requirements of ISO 9001:2008.

Using a process approach to define his processes, Bob had no trouble complying with the above requirements. Bob's core processes were defined and documented sensibly, while measurable process objectives were established for each, as well as for the system of processes. Activity-level objectives were also established in support of process objectives. (Several were already in place, but their relationship to process and system objectives were not clear until the processes and system were appropriately defined.) After that, it was a matter of measuring performance relative to stated objectives, identifying where improvements can be made, taking actions to improve performance, and repeating these support processes routinely.

Every future revision of ISO 9001 will endorse use of a process approach with increasing emphasis until the concept is widely understood and applied by organizations and auditors alike. It's simply the right way to do it.

To Bob, parting advice might include the following:

> If you ever pursue certification to AS9100 or ISO 13485 or ISO/TS 16949, etc., apply the same approach as you did with your core processes. First, understand the sector scheme requirements and determine how they apply to your operations. Recognize the degree to which existing processing meets requirements and go from there. Where possible, integrate new processing requirements complying with additional external requirements into your existing processes and process documentation as necessary.

> Avoid the temptation to automatically raise a new QMS process (and procedure) for each additional sector scheme requirement or clause, and consider instead addressing them in process fashion. This way, more procedures are not necessarily needed to address additional external requirements. Instead,

more robust procedures might be in order—procedures complying with a wider variety of requirements.

For example, some organizations might address risk requirements with a support process called Risk Management. These organizations would then recognize a new QMS support process. Other organizations might view risk management activities as being resident in each QMS process. Here, risk management is not viewed as being a process; it is integrated into QMS processes.

One organization might make process owners responsible for risk management. Another might manage risk in association with each project, requiring participation from management of each process involved with the project. Still another company might choose to include risk management as part of management review. As long as the planned arrangements are effective, the requirements have been adequately addressed.

Once processes are robust enough to be effective in meeting requirements, and they are documented accordingly, insist that CB audits are performed in terms of company procedures, in keeping with a process approach. A process-based audit checklist—one based upon your own compliant procedures—is better at assessing conformity to management's planned arrangements vis-à-vis ISO 9001. And it's done without unduly stressing and confusing personnel with "ISOese."

Generally, management personnel seem to like things that make sense. But as ISO 9001 is so often rolled out with a standard-based spin, it understandably makes no sense to management. "ISO responsibilities," including oversight and operation of the QMS, become something to be delegated, insulating top management from the QMS. Although the involvement of top management is required of ISO 9001, this involvement is all too often like the system itself: a confusing formality laden with unnecessary paperwork.

The Process Approach of ISO 9001

Using the process approach, quality management no longer consists of confusing "ISOese." The language of quality is properly spoken every day by those whose work affects quality. If you haven't adopted a process approach, take back your management system and define it in your own terms. Adopting a process approach is not difficult. It makes life easier. More important, it's the right thing to do for the sake of quality.

Anticipated Revisions

Future revisions to the standard will not likely have a significant impact on the process approach as described in this book. Future revisions to this book will accommodate new voicing of requirements to apply a process approach in future revisions of ISO 9001.